BEST RADIO
PLAYS OF 1981

BEST RADIO PLAYS OF 1981

The Giles Cooper Award Winners

Peter Barnes: The Jumping Mimuses of Byzantium
Don Haworth: Talk of Love and War
Harold Pinter: Family Voices
David Pownall: Beef
John P. Rooney: The Dead Image
Paul Thain: The Biggest Sandcastle in the World

METHUEN LONDON/BBC PUBLICATIONS

This collection first published in Great Britain in 1982 by Methuen London Ltd, 11 New Fetter Lane, London EC4P 4EE and BBC Publications, 35 Marylebone High Street, London W1M 4AA.

The Jumping Mimuses of Byzantium first published by Heinemann Educational Books Ltd., in 1981 in *The Collected Plays of Peter Barnes*.

Family Voices first published by Next Editions in 1981 and subsequently by Eyre Methuen Ltd., in 1981 in *Pinter Plays: Four*.

Set in IBM 10pt Journal by 𝍏 Tek-Art, Croydon, Surrey
Printed in Great Britain by Richard Clay (The Chaucer Press) Ltd, Bungay, Suffolk.

ISBN 0 413 50290 2

CONTENTS

THE GILES COOPER AWARDS: a note on the selection

Giles Cooper

When the BBC and Methuen first discussed the setting up of awards for outstanding writing in radio drama, the name of Giles Cooper was very quickly proposed as among the most suitable to characterise the awards and to symbolise the qualities we sought to encourage. He was chosen from among a number of distinguished dramatists because of the range and inventiveness of his radio work. Invariably subtle and rich in layers of implication, his writing was always accessible and entertaining; his plays transferred to other media but they were supreme in radio, which Cooper used to the full as an art form in its own right. The awards that bear his name are designed to encourage others to do the same.

Eligibility

Eligible for the awards was every original radio play first broadcast by the BBC domestic service from December 1980 to December 1981 (almost 500 plays in total). Excluded from consideration were translations, adaptations and dramatised 'features'. In making their selection, the judges took account of the very wide range both of length and subject matter within the BBC's output, though it was decided that the final selection should not necessarily represent all of the established programme 'slots' on Radios 3 and 4.

Selection

The editors of each of the drama 'slots', in consultation with individual producers, prepared an initial list of plays for the judges' consideration. Their combined suggestions, numbering over 40 plays in all, formed the basis of the judges' shortlist, though each of the judges was entitled to nominate further plays from his or her own listening during the year. In the event, the selection was made from 51 plays read by all the judges. The deciding factor throughout was the quality of the writing, for which this award is made, and not the part played in the final broadcast by acting or production.

Judges

The judges for the 1981 awards were:
  Martin Esslin, Professor of Drama, Stanford University, California and
      ex-head of BBC Radio Drama
  Nicholas Hern, Drama Editor, Methuen
  Richard Imison, Script Editor, BBC Radio Drama
  Gillian Reynolds, radio critic, *The Daily Telegraph*

PREFACE

The radio play is a curious beast. It may be of any length and take an almost infinite variety of forms. At the moment of its creation — that is to say when a certain orchestration of sounds and silences emerge from some form of loudspeaker and enter the listener's head — it is an experience at once so intimate and so subjective that it is doubtful whether two people would agree precisely on what they had heard, let alone seen in their mind's eye as a result.

Over the years, and across the world, confusion has perhaps been worse confounded by the multiplicity of uses to which the medium of radio has been put in the service of different forms of dramatic experience. Whether ideally suited to the purpose or not, radio can undoubtedly be used simply as a carrier of essentially theatrical experience to a mass audience. For example, long before the advent on the South Bank of a more concrete temple for the celebration of our dramatic heritage, radio's national theatre of the air introduced more people to more stage plays from different ages and countries than any other medium. As a matter of fact, it still does.

Elsewhere, radio's facility as a cheap and flexible purveyor of vicarious experience has been used to extend other existing traditions. In America, it became a logical extension of vaudeville and popular fiction. There, the term 'radio drama' became synonymous for many people with the *Lux Mystery Theater, The Jack Benny Show* or *The Lone Ranger*. In Britain too, the home-grown thriller serials and 'soap operas' such as *Dick Barton, The Dales* and *The Archers* owed much more at their inception to familiar forms of serialisation in publishing and the cinema than to any specific concept of the art of radio. Ironically, when that art began to be explored in earnest throughout the world, it was almost as a conscious reaction to radio 'drama' as it was then known.

Yet in the course of the past fifty-eight years of broadcasting; ever since Richard Hughes completed the first original 'listening-play', *Danger,* in 1924, the radio play has emerged as a separate, vital and genuinely creative art form, and has continued to thrive and diversify. It has defied competition and survived neglect. It has overridden fashion and fed on the challenge of new ideas. It has, I think, learnt to draw nourishment from its coexisting forms: from the stage play, the dramatic reading, the adaptation; from the feature and the documentary, and from poetry. And it must be said that it has influenced all of these in its turn.

All the while, the radio play has remained a curious phenomenon. It is the only dramatic form uniquely tailored to the taste, experience — even the mood — of the individual listener; certainly not guaranteed to satisfy them but actually arising from them as well as from the art of its creators. In a pure form, it is a single voice with an arresting tale to tell or an emotion to share. The line between the spoken story and the true dramatic monologue is a narrow one but it exists and in the form which is a play the listener is drawn closer into involvement with the voice that he hears, ideally to the point where it seems to be his own, even when speaking of things he does not know.

At the other extreme, the radio play acts as an instant magic carpet between centuries and continents. The excitement expressed as long ago as 1932 by Lance Sieveking in *The Stuff of Radio* when he wrote of operating the dramatic control panel like playing a mighty organ, conjuring up orchestras and crowds, poetry and battles with equal facility, was not just the over-enthusiasm of a creative pioneer with a new technical toy. Epic radio can still be enormously satisfying, though it needs extraordinary skill and precision on the part of all concerned — the writer perhaps most of all.

In between, the radio play offers the writer some simple rules, and a bewildering range of opportunity for their subtle application. It is a medium relatively easy to enter yet which would take more than a lifetime to explore in full. Giles Cooper opened many doors in a brilliant, too brief, career. The plays in this volume open some more. May they inspire other writers, whether new in the business or already introduced to the awesome joys of radio drama, to take us further still.

Richard Imison
(January 1982)

THE JUMPING MIMUSES OF BYZANTIUM

by Peter Barnes

Peter Barnes has written widely for the stage, film and radio. His plays include *Sclerosis* (Royal Shakespeare Company, Aldwych Theatre); *The Ruling Class* (Nottingham and Piccadilly Theatres, also filmed); *Leonardo's Last Supper* (Open Space Theatre); *Noonday Demons* (Open Space); *The Bewitched* (RSC, Aldwych) and *Laughter!* (Royal Court Theatre). His adaptations include Jonson's *The Devil is an Ass* (Edinburgh Festival and National Theatre); Wedekind's *Lulu* (Nottingham, Royal Court and Apollo); Jonson's *Bartholomew Fair* (Round House, London); Feydeau's and Wedekind's *The Frontiers of Farce* (Old Vic and Criterion Theatres); Brecht's and Wedekind's *For All Those Who Get Despondent* (Royal Court); Marston's *Antonio* (Nottingham) and Wedekind's *The Devil Himself* (Lyric Theatre, Hammersmith), all of which he also directed.

The Jumping Mimuses of Byzantium was first broadcast on BBC Radio 3 on 20th September 1981, with John Clements.

Producer: Ian Cotterell

MAYA. I'm dying now. But that's good. I'm an old man and my life has been spent preparing for this moment: to live well and to die better. My early years were filled with prayer and fasting. I often slept for just one or two hours a night and lived on five olives and muddy water — and walked barefoot in the snow in the depths of winter.

I was born in a village to the north of Amin near Byzantium. God-possessed, I became a disciple of Paul the Hermit who lived in a cave near Kharhut. He always urged me not to overdo my self-mortification. 'There's too much pride in too much humility' he would say. But I was young and confident. I went to Egypt, then the chief school of asceticism, where I visited various longhaired penitents who scourged their flesh in praising God. At the time I was a firm Monophysite, a religious sect, out of favour with the authorities. The Emperor Justinian had me and others like me, driven from our monkish cells. Some went further into the desert, but I took a ship to Byzantium. Bearded, I bearded the Emperor and his Empress, Theodora, in their court. Filthy and tattered I strode into that gilded throne room and cried: 'Carrion of Satan, hellspawn! Persecutors of men of God, may your womb be blasted and your instrument of procreation drop off!' Looking back, it was an act of overweening pride. I was right but presumptuous to swear at those presumptuous rulers.

Neither Justinian nor Theodora were able to reply to my holy zeal in the usual way — with violence. For one thing, we Monophysites were still a powerful party in Byzantium and they had a superstitious awe of anyone who spoke the truth. Theodora wanted me to become her confessor, but I told her her burden of sin was too great for one man to cope with. She tried to bribe me with a hundred pounds of gold but I flung the bag away with one hand shouting, 'To hell with you and the money you use to tempt me.' All were amazed at my strength and the fact that it was money I was throwing away. A rare sight in Byzantium or anywhere else for that matter.

Afterwards I went to live in the hills outside the city. The Empress sent me a message saying she would be glad to supply whatever I wished. I replied that she need not suppose herself to have anything a true servant of God could use, unless it was the fear of God, if she had ever possessed such a thing as that.

Living in a cave in the mountains and eating wild fruit and herbs, I was credited with at least three miracles. Though they were commonplace around Byzantium at the time, I gained the reputation of being a Saint, not, I fear, through my piety, but because I once spoke the truth to an Emperor and rejected an Empress's bribe. Naturally I was consulted on religious and ethical matters. I delivered hundreds of judgements on the right way for a Christian to live and die. I was very sure I knew the truth of God's mind. Of course I was plagued with Satanic visions but for a man like me Satan's easily dealt with.

But this isn't the story I want written down, to bridge the time between now and when: now, here in Amin, 542, dying, and when you read these words.

One day in the year 530 there appeared on the streets of Amin a performer, a Merry Andrew, a clown — what we call a Jumping Mimus. He had a female assistant with him. Dressed in brightly patched costumes and bells, they juggled with coloured balls, leaped and tumbled; the young man jested and the young girl sang. As was the custom, she also seemed to carry on her trade as a prostitute. Unfortunately such immorality was not unique amongst us. Though we have a reputation for fanatical piety, it goes hand in hand with a rampant sensuality.

Though the people had seen Merry Andrews before, this pair attracted special attention because of their extreme youth and beauty. The young man had an agile body and wit. The young girl sang suggestively:
'By day my eyes, by night my soul desires thee
Weary I lie alone
Once in a dream it seemed you were beside me
Oh if you would only come.'

The two were given money and abused. They were liked for their skill and hated for their freedom. Every evening the Jumping Mimuses would disappear, nobody knew where.

Certain Court officials, who were living in Amin at the time, saw them performing and, struck by the beauty of the young girl, went to the Governor and asked him to officially declare her a prostitute. That way they could enjoy her favours in a state brothel. Such is the depraved trade of the court, I only wonder they did not try to arrange a similar fate for the young man. However, the Governor's wife heard of the matter and being a strong-minded God-fearing woman saw to it that the court officials left with their vile tails hanging limply between their legs. She had the young girl brought to her and advised her to lead a better life. The girl listened attentively and went straight back to her companion in sin.

But the Governor's wife was not satisfied. There was something mysterious about the girl. She consulted a friend of mine, John of Ephesus, about the pair. After a great deal of trouble he found they lived in a small hut on some scrub-land on the edge of the town.

One night he paid them a surprise visit. He stumbled across to the hut and saw through the open window, by the light of a solitary oil lamp, the two still in their brightly coloured costumes, on their knees praying. John of Ephesus watched them for at least an hour at their prayers. Then he confronted them. Why did they pray so devoutly? Why did they behave so wantonly in the streets by day and devote themselves to prayer at night? The young couple refused to answer.

I was in Amin at the time, offering up prayers for the soul of Paul the Hermit. John of Ephesus asked me to help him to try to unravel the mystery of the Merry Andrews. Secret devotion and public wantonness seemed to me unique whilst the reverse was all too common. So I found myself one stormy night stumbling across the scrub-land to find the young couple. I knew it to be a dangerous part of Amin. Sure enough, that very night two ruffians sprang out of the darkness threatening to rob me. On most other occasions I would have remonstrated with them on their lack of Christian feeling, but this time, I confess, I felt ill-tempered for being out on such a night instead of praying in my monk's cell. So I gave them a vivid demonstration of what can be done by the power of Christ when conjoined with a strong right arm by breaking the leg of one sinner and the pelvis of the other before they fled.

As I approached the hut I saw the light from the open window. Inside the two were kneeling on the earth floor, facing each other, their hands clasped in prayer. Their costumes, pale blue, red and yellow, glowed in a golden light. The girl's face was without a blemish, her eyes were clear as a summer day.

But I was not to be seduced by pretty pictures. I burst in unannounced. I must have been a disturbing sight, standing six-foot three in what was left of my stockings, matted hair over my shoulders, grey beard bristling — Jehovah come to punish the world for its sins. After all I had frightened Emperors and Empresses, but these two young sinners rose quietly, the young man offering me some bread while the young girl poured water for me.

I told them why I was there and that I would not leave until I had discovered the truth about them. They saw I was determined so they asked me to sit on the only chair in the room whilst they squatted on the floor in front of me and told their story.

The young man spoke first. He said that their names were Theophilus

and Mary. I believed that, she looked like a Mary — the Mary of
the Gospel, but which Mary of the Gospel — Magdalene or Mother of
Christ? Each was an only child of rich and noble families in the city
of Antioch. They were to be married. But one night when
Theophilus was fifteen he found a poor man in his father's stable,
hiding in the straw to keep warm. Around this poor man's mouth
and hands was a halo which only Theophilus could see and which
disappeared whenever the servants entered. This I thought rather
convenient, but I said nothing.

The holy man said his name was Procopius and he had come from
Rome. He had fled from his home on the day of his wedding to
escape marriage in order to serve God. He then predicted the exact
date of the death of Theophilus' parents and also Mary's, which
would be soon after. Mary came to see him and he told the young
couple that when their parents died they were to sell everything
they had and give the money to the poor and live consecrated lives.

I was impressed but suspicious. Certain elements of their story were
familiar: children of a rich family, meeting a holy stranger, in the
stable — usually it was St Alexus — giving away all their possessions
to the poor. These were the basic ingredients of legend. They could
be true, but they were familiar to all Christians.

Mary continued the story. They were instructed to live a holy life
consecrated to God but in disguise. No one was to know of it. So
when their parents died on the date predicted, they disguised themselves as Merry Andrews, Jumping Mimuses and travelled throughout
the East. They lived in virginity together, whilst in the eyes of the
world they wallowed in sin — two shameful wantons, companions in
debauchery. I looked into Mary's beautiful face; could I find the
truth there? Were they saints, reviling, degrading their flesh for the
glory of God? Had these two beautiful people reached the peak of
asceticism? An ascetic who, by means of prayer and fasting, was
completely dead to the temptation of the world had no longer to
fear the world. He or she need no longer run away, their inner
cleansing was so complete that they would give themselves up to
licentiousness without sin or risk, since they were no longer subject
to passion and so could indulge in wantonness. They were ascetics
beyond asceticism. Saint Salus, the dissolute saint, drank, ate and
was one day seen leaving a prostitute's room looking furtively
around him so as to increase suspicion. Saints like that have so
conquered passion and so triumphed over nature that no glance or
touch can rouse them to any dishonourable action. The Grace of
God combined in them the most contrary elements which would
otherwise be incompatible. Could Theophilus and Mary be of that
breed? We solitaries had gone into the desert to find purity, solitude
and God, now the experiment was turning full circle, with a return
to the world. Who would have thought these two performers,
prostituting themselves in the streets of Amin were saints?

I took Mary's face in my hands and looked for the truth there. Yes, such beauty was saintlike. She told me the degradation of her flesh was an offering to Christ. She sang again, clear and true:
'By day my eyes, by night my soul desires thee
Weary I lie alone.
Once in a dream it seemed you were beside me
Oh if you would only come.'

She explained the 'thee' was Christ. The song was a desire for Christ's love to come to her.

We prayed together all night. I bearded, gnarled, hardened by the sun, they bright and soft, with the beauty of youth. I left in the morning and they continued performing in the streets of Amin where their fame and mystery made them even more popular; they attracted crowds wherever they went.

When I was looking into the eyes of Mary, the truth seemed obvious. As obvious as the truth had always been to me. Later I had my doubts. But by that time they had gone. They suddenly vanished. I never saw them again. John of Ephesus met them once on the road to Byzantium and I heard years later they bought a villa outside Antioch, though another story had it they both took Holy Orders.

Were they telling the truth? Were they sinners for Christ? Or just tricksters who knew our love of new and exotic forms of worship? Was she a prostitute with a new perversion — sanctity? Or an ascetic with a new discipline — fornication? And with these doubts came others. If I couldn't divine the truth of a pair of common Merry Andrews, how could I divine God's truth?

Earning a little money by making mats and baskets of palm leaves, I built a hut and planted a garden. Men and women still came to me, but I gave them food now instead of advice. On the outbreak of the plague of '42, I looked after the sick and forced the Emperor to help the victims with food, clothes and shelter. There was work to do and the days of my solitude were over. But not the endless war between truth and lies, half-truths and half-lies, lies and lies. In this world there's no break between truth and lies, they are joined: did she lie by swearing she lay with men for Christ's sake? And who was she lying to if she lied?

You'll say, reading this: 'Stupid holy fool — or just plain old fool — of course they were lying. They tricked you. You made them famous.'

Yes, that may be true. I'll soon know, absorbed into the universal mind of God who knows all things. It wouldn't surprise me to discover they were two tricksters, but I held her face in my hands and looked into her eyes . . . pretty picture . . . the light and the face, and the bright costumes in the flame . . .

Of course I'll enter God's house, sit on His right hand, meet the disciples and the archangel Gabriel and bathe in everlasting light, but I confess above all I'm dying to know the truth about the Jumping Mimuses of Byzantium . . .

TALK OF LOVE AND WAR

by Don Haworth

To Rob

Don Haworth was born at Bacup, Lancashire, served in the Royal Air Force and worked as a journalist in print and radio in several parts of the world. He joined BBC Television as a news-reporter, became a producer on the old *Tonight* and later *Panorama*, and is now a documentary producer based at Manchester. His film, *Fred Dibnah, Steeplejack*, won the British Academy Award for documentary in 1980. He is the first writer of radio plays to win a second Giles Cooper Award. The first was for *Episode on a Thursday Evening* in 1978. In 1976 he won the Society of Authors' Award for *On a Day in Summer in a Garden* and in 1977 the award of the West German Academy for Performance Arts for *Events at the Salamander Hotel*. A collection of his earlier radio plays, *We All Come to it in the End*, was published in 1972.

Talk of Love and War was first broadcast on BBC Radio 3 on
29th November 1981. The cast was as follows:

TOM   William Nighy
JAMES   Hugh Ross
Director: Richard Wortley

Time: early 1944. Tom as narrator is telling the story only a little time,
perhaps two years, after it happened.

The drone of many heavy bombers, and muffled drumming of anti-aircraft fire. A faster aircraft passes close, followed by a burst of cannon and machine gun fire and an explosion.

TOM (*narration*). James and I flew night-fighters on intruder operations over Western Europe, and we lived in a cubicle of a corrugated hut which we shared with an iron stove. Both the stove and James were out when I got back from leave, so I went to bed and was well asleep when James came in.

Door thrown open. Light switched on.

JAMES (*surprised*). Tom! Sorry to disturb you.

TOM. That's OK.

Door closed.

JAMES (*pleased*). You weren't due back today. What like a leave did you have?

TOM. Fine.

JAMES. Grand to see you.

TOM. Grand to see you.

They both laugh at the pleasure of each other.

TOM. Anything happened?

JAMES. They've stuck a tannoy on a pole outside our hut.

TOM. Oh Christ.

JAMES. And my nav Bill Slater's bust his ankle playing football.

TOM. Can he hobble?

JAMES. Fine.

TOM. That's OK then. Navigators don't fly with their feet.

JAMES. That's what he says. He flies with his head.

TOM. Navs all have big heads. You can pick out their caps on the pegs.

JAMES. He's growing a moustache.

TOM. He'll look like a pork butcher.

JAMES. He does.

TOM. In fact they'd be better totally legless. They'd take up less room.

JAMES (*laughs*). I'm glad you had a good leave.

TOM. Fine.

JAMES (*pleased*). Grand.

TOM. It was piss poor really.

JAMES. Nobody home you knew?

TOM. No. I dug the allotment and took my mother to the pictures twice. She's sent you some rock buns.

JAMES. That's good of her.

TOM. It wasn't piss poor really. Just sort of —

JAMES. Moderate.

TOM. Yes. So I came back. What you all bulled up for?

JAMES. How?

TOM. Best uniform. Where've you been?

JAMES. Out.

TOM (*after a pause*). How many ops have you done while I was away?

JAMES. Just the one.

TOM. The one?

JAMES. The one that was scrubbed the night before you went. We did it a couple of nights later.

TOM. And since then?

JAMES. Nothing. We've had three scrubbed on account of weather.

TOM. It was all right where I was.

JAMES. Apparently it wasn't all right where we were going.

TOM. So the whole war effort has ground to a halt in my absence?

JAMES. I believe the Chiefs of Staff were drafting a letter requesting your return.

TOM. So what of the victory for which people of all beliefs and none so fervently pray?

JAMES. More doubtful.

TOM. And the peace for which all hearts yearn?

JAMES. More remote.

Pause, then they both laugh.

TOM. Did you find that mobile fighter beacon where we got in among them?

JAMES. They changed frequency.

TOM. They do — every fifteen minutes. We had it plotted for Christ's sake. I told Andy to get a fix.

JAMES. A cocked hat.

TOM. All right, a cocked hat.

JAMES. It was a rather large cocked hat.

TOM. How large?

JAMES (*laughs*). Took in about half of eastern Belgium.

TOM. Good God.

JAMES *laughs.*

How many did you shoot down?

JAMES. Six.

TOM. And that's what our respected intelligence officer wrote in his report?

JAMES. No . . . One probable. (*He laughs.*)

TOM. Very sound, old George. He can see through a pack of wild claims. It's his legal experience as a solicitor, having dealt in court with galleries of lying criminals.

JAMES. Thank you.

TOM. Not at all . . . Oh, I got a scarf for you. In my grip.

JAMES. Will I open it?

TOM. Sure.

Grip unzipped.

Take your pick. My mother got two off an old bird who organises knitting for the Merchant Navy.

JAMES. Bang on. Pity to deprive the seadogs though. Did you know there's only eighteen inches freeboard on a loaded tanker?

TOM. I don't have your access to the factual Scottish newspapers. The rock buns are in the red tin.

Tin opened.

JAMES. Whizzo. Very kind of your old lady.

Silence.

TOM. OK, how about bounding into your pit and getting the light out? I've had a hard day on the railway.

JAMES. Fine . . . I've something to tell you.

JAMES (*after a pause*). It'll maybe wait till morning.

TOM. Go on now you've started.

JAMES. Tim Unwin and Roger Jackson bought it.

TOM. How?

JAMES. There was a Halifax squirming about, coned in searchlights, and some Lancasters and Halifaxes steered into the dark area above the crossed beams and a couple of Me 110s went in after them and Tim went in after the Me's. A Lanc and a Halifax went up in flames and another heavy went down — or possibly it was a 110.

TOM (*ironically*). They don't look all that much alike.

JAMES. I only got a glimpse. It wasn't burning too well when I lost sight. Then Tim and Roger went up.

TOM. You saw it was them?

JAMES. Only a Mossie goes up like that.

TOM. No parachutes?

JAMES. No time. Just wuff.

TOM. What hit 'em?

JAMES. Don't know. Bill thought the 110s had cleared by then, so maybe they were hit by our own heavies.

TOM. Standard practice.

JAMES. Or maybe the flak lifted above the searchlight beams.

TOM. It's a played-out move . . . I never managed to talk to Tim much.

JAMES. Buttoned-up bloke. Bad time as a wee lad, I believe. He joined up as a boy apprentice way back.

TOM. Did he have no parents?

JAMES. Something like that.

TOM. So what's happened to his personal clobber?

JAMES. Old Harry's coping.

TOM. Roger was married.

JAMES. They found a stack of letters in his locker from a young lady in Wisbech.

TOM. He was getting on in years for that kind of thing.

JAMES. Twenty-six. He'd done a tour on Lancs, of course.

TOM. So what happened about her? They couldn't send the official *billet doux* to two ladies, could they?

JAMES. Old Harry drafted a letter that wouldn't be compromising for one of the blokes to send her, you know, Dear Madam, I am writing to the friends and acquaintances of the late lamented Roger Jackson to impart the sad tidings, etc. Andy wrote it.

TOM. I hope he made a better job of it than he did of his cocked-up cocked hat.

JAMES. He only had to copy out what old Harry wrote.

TOM. That's about his level . . . Have we got a replacement aircraft?

JAMES. None arrived.

TOM. What's being done about it?

JAMES. I don't know. You're the flight commander.

TOM. I've been on leave for Christ's sake.

JAMES. You're back now. (*He laughs.*)

TOM. Come on, James, get out of your Sunday suit and let's have the light off.

JAMES. Sorry.

We hear sounds of JAMES *preparing for bed — washing, teeth cleaning, alarm clock winding — during the following dialogue.*

TOM. He'd have made a good pilot, Tim Unwin.

JAMES. Nice bloke. Sort of loner by nature.

TOM. I could never really talk to him.

JAMES. He didn't talk. Even old Harry didn't get him to talk.

TOM. Thing is, his flying was correct. He stuck to the book. C.O. said to me one day, Isn't he rather lacking in flair?

JAMES. He's a bloody goon. I believe he earned his crust before the war flying biplanes in an air circus.

TOM. That's what he claims. Actually he was ringmaster of a flea circus.

JAMES *laughs.*

No, a bloke like Tim who flies correctly develops flair. He needs the luck to have the time.

JAMES. Sure.

TOM. I've seen enough of these cowboys who finish in a smoking heap because they've too much flair and panache to remember to re-set the bloody altimeter.

JAMES. Yep . . . OK for lights out?

TOM. Been OK for nearly an hour.

JAMES. Fine. (*Click of light switch. Uncertainly:*) Tom.

TOM (*sleepily*). Yes.

JAMES. I've something else to tell you.

TOM. Go on.

JAMES. I'm going to get married.

TOM. Who to?

JAMES. WAAF sergeant in the post office.

TOM. Blond girl?

JAMES. No, dark. Welsh.

TOM (*yawning*). I haven't a very good memory for faces.

JAMES. No . . . I'll tell you about it tomorrow.

TOM (*sleepily*). Uh, uh. I'll look forward to hearing . . . Did you put the lid back on the rock buns?

JAMES. Yes . . . Goodnight, Tom.

TOM: Goodnight, James.

Alarm clock ticks.

TOM (*narration*). I should say something about the third inhabitant of our abode, the iron stove, which, although inanimate, was the centre of our life as a dog may be in a civilian residence. It was lined with fireclay, out of which James had chipped a panel so that a rectangle in the outer casing glowed when the stove was going, and we made toast on non-operational nights with bread stolen from the mess. Some evenings we played ping-pong or billiards, but often we were sufficiently clapped out to be content to sit on our beds and read or listen to the wireless. James actually never read much except *Tee Emm,* which was a comic magazine designed to convey training memoranda in an appealing form, and the papers from home, which had columns of such facts as the number of inches of freeboard on a loaded tanker and jokes reflecting the keen Scottish interest in drunkenness, football and domestic disharmony. This, in the days before his thoughts turned to marriage, left his mind free to work up hypochondria about his aircraft.

JAMES. You know this intermittence in fuel transfer I have from the drop tank to the starboard outer wing tank.

TOM (*ironically*). I believe I have heard you mention it.

JAMES. I had a talk to Alec today.

TOM. Which Alec?

JAMES. Engineering officer. You know it isn't a pukka cross feed.

TOM. So I'm told.

JAMES. It works on air pressure from the outlet side of an engine vacuum pump.

TOM. I'm prepared to believe it.

JAMES. But I understand from Alec that the feeds in both the port and starboard wings are worked from the port engine.

TOM. OK, if he says so.

JAMES. It seems a lopsided system.

TOM. Write a snotty letter to de Havilands.

JAMES. It might account, though, for the fact that I only get this trouble on the starboard side.

TOM. It might well. How about putting the kettle on and trying a transfer into the teapot?

JAMES. Sure.

JAMES. What's that you're reading?

TOM. Book old Harry put me on to — Proust.

JAMES. Literary?

TOM. Very.

JAMES. He's a well clued-up bloke, old Harry.

TOM. He's a good adjutant.

JAMES. He was a Regular, wasn't he? Where did he learn to read?

TOM. They chucked him out when he bust up his leg and he'd bugger-all to do for several years but read books.

JAMES. What's it about?

TOM. Love, jealousy — that sort of thing.

JAMES. Aye.

TOM. It's hard to say really. There's twelve volumes of it and old Harry only has two and seven.

JAMES. That's sparse.

TOM. But he's hoping with the help of God to knock off several volumes they have in the station library at West Croxford.

JAMES. Must be difficult for you, sorting it out.

TOM. Especially as they're very long sentences and if you're interrupted in the middle of one you've got to go back to the beginning. It's more like playing snakes and ladders than reading a bloody book.

JAMES. I'm sorry.

TOM. Not at all. I want it to last till old Harry knocks off the other volumes then I'll whip through the whole caboodle in the proper order.

JAMES. If you're spared.

TOM. Another snag old Harry mentioned, the bloke who wrote it was queer.

JAMES. Is it about sodomy?

TOM. No. It's about men and women. But being clued-up only about queers, he simply transferred their relationships to normal people which apparently is misleading.

JAMES. They should have sent him on a conversion course.

He pours water into teapot.

I don't think I've ever met a queer.

TOM. You wouldn't. They're all in the Navy.

TOM (*narration*). One day our stove, which was an indispensable companion on those evenings, suffered a nasty accident. Aircraftman Harold Lusty was charged with the duties of awakening us at unusual hours, which he did well, of keeping squalor at bay in our abode, which he did moderately well, and with lighting the stove at permitted times, which was utterly beyond his ability. We would come back to find the stove out and the air filled with smoke and floating scraps of burned paper. One day he completely blackened our den.

JAMES *laughing.*

TOM. What is it?

JAMES. Before you go in brace yourself.

TOM *opens the door.*

TOM. What the hell's happened?

JAMES (*laughing*). He tried to light the stove with petrol.

TOM. Is he all right?

JAMES. Except his nerves.

TOM. I'll fix his nerves. I'll put him on a fizzer. He'll get 112 days.

JAMES. That's what he said.

TOM. Said what?

JAMES. You'd put him on a fizzer and he'd get 112 days.

TOM. Where is he now?

JAMES. Gone into hiding.

TOM (*indignant*). The place is running with water.

JAMES (*laughing*). His prompt action with the stirrup pump when the flames were licking round the walls.

TOM. Our beds are saturated. He's deliberately hosed 'em down. I'll have him shot.

JAMES. He said you'd have him shot.

TOM. By way of accepting his fate?

JAMES. No. By way of proposing an alternative.

TOM. Which is what?

JAMES. That I should shepherd you to a remote place so he might return privily and in safety and renew his efforts to light the stove as a means of counteracting the dowsing that followed his earlier attempt.

He laughs at the situation and also at TOM's *irritation.*

TOM (*narration*). Thereafter James took it upon himself to light the stove. A stream of visitors came to view the squalor of our abode. Mess guests were brought, visiting concert artistes, and even a couple of army officers. Old Harry, who at once time had preserved the peace on the North West frontier of India by bombing native villages, said that in all his travels he had never enjoyed the privilege of viewing so squalid a den nor even read of one in his many excursions into the world's literature. But we painted it up and under James' care our stove thrived so greatly that those who had derided our abode now craved licence to come and make toast. James' navigator, Bill Slater, was a great toast-maker — and so until his untimely demise was Roger Jackson when not absent on operations or, as it transpired, visiting his lady friend at Wisbech.

JAMES. Alec said he might drop in tonight.

TOM. I reckon our abode has become the social centre of the whole station.

JAMES. Gale and Hemsdale get more visitors.

TOM. Fair do's. They've half a hut to start with and a couple of good armchairs they got from home.

JAMES. Gale and Hemsdale, they *sound* like a furniture shop.

TOM. Quite.

JAMES. I believe they've acquired a chamber pot.

TOM. They lack nothing.

JAMES. No.

TOM (*pause, then with emphasis*). Except our stove.

JAMES. Quite.

TOM. And your superb handling thereof.

JAMES. Thank you.

TOM. Your flying leaves much to be desired but your stove handling is unequalled throughout the command.

JAMES. They've had a go at chipping the lining off their stove for toast making.

TOM. What happened?

JAMES (*laughing*). The whole bloody lot fell in.

They both laugh.

TOM. Whizzo. Bang-on.

JAMES. So that when they get it roaring it glows like an exhaust stack.

They both laugh.

JAMES. And gives all their visitors a foretaste of hell.

They both laugh with joy.

TOM. It's like in this book I'm reading.

JAMES. Comrade Proust?

TOM. Yep. Different people have salons and compete for custom. Well, there's a pair of turds called Verdurin and they regularly get a football crowd but only vulgar types, you know, all the scum and riff-raff.

JAMES. That sounds very much like Gale and Hemsdale. Dickie, your nav, goes.

TOM. Exactly, that makes the point. He's a good nav, but he keeps low company. He patronises pubs full of whores and spivs. Whereas our place by contrast strongly resembles the salon of the Duchesse de Guermantes.

JAMES. That has the right ring about it.

TOM. Aristocratic old bint, and if any of the riff-raff saunter in they get the bum's rush, head over heels down the grand staircase, no messing.

JAMES. If Gale and Hemsdale get the chop we'll maybe move into their room smartish.

TOM. Hadn't thought of that.

JAMES. And as they fly together —

TOM. Two birds with one stone.

They laugh.

JAMES. But we'll take our stove.

TOM. Isn't it cemented in?

JAMES. I could cope.

TOM. In fact, thinking more positively about it, if we see 'em go up in flames we'll execute an 180 degree turn forthwith and nip back and shift the stove and our clobber into their premises while other claimants are still embroiled with the enemy.

JAMES. We could get shot for that.

TOM. It'd be worth it.

JAMES. Then thinking even more positively still, you might help to bring about this happy turn of events by leading them into the hairbrained forays you normally reserve for me.

TOM. You're up for a gong.

JAMES. I'd prefer their hut and a lease of life to enjoy it.

TOM. I believe old Harry's going to get something about your stove handling written into your citation.

JAMES. Very decent of him.

TOM. And your old man'll be able to wear his kilt and topper outside Buckingham Palace and your mother'll no doubt get a new hat out of it.

JAMES. Which is fine but doesn't get us Gale and Hemsdale's hut.

TOM. No . . . I'll bear in mind what you propose about sending them to their deaths.

JAMES. Instead of always chucking me in. Just wean yourself from the habit.

TOM. I'll try to.

JAMES. Hemsdale started a conversation in the mess which was interrupted but I think he was working round to permission to come and toast at our stove.

TOM (*taken aback*). To come and toast here?

JAMES. I think that's what he was after.

TOM (*pause, then judicially*). Well, I don't think we'd actually deny a toasting licence to anybody in the squadron.

JAMES. And they're nice blokes, Gale and Hemsdale, apart from hogging the most palatial premises.

TOM. But the etiquette of it. I mean they're proprietors of a rival salon.

JAMES. They shouldn't ask to use our stove.

TOM. Quite. And we won't ask to use their po.

TOM (*narration*). The day after I got back from leave I intended to have a long lie in bed but the incendiarist Aircraftman Lusty woke me up clattering round with his buckets and brooms and the new tannoy outside the hut, endlessly speaking tin sentences, made further sleep impossible. It was like living on a dog track. So I got up and cycled round, having a look at the aircraft and hobnobbing with people, which in the end took longer than a proper working day. When I got back James had lighted the stove and left the bread in its proper place under my shirts but was nowhere to be seen. He came in at 10.30.

Door opens and closes.

JAMES. Hi.

TOM. Where've you been?

JAMES. Out — with the young lady I told you about.

TOM. Who was that?

JAMES. The one I'm going to marry.

TOM. Straight up?

JAMES. Yes.

TOM (*pause*). You did tell me. I'm sorry, James, I didn't take it in. I was dozing off.

JAMES. The WAAF sergeant in the post office. She's called Gwyneth.

TOM. Most charming. I've often noticed her.

JAMES (*laughing*). You haven't, but it's good of you to say so. It may seem a bit sudden to you.

TOM. No . . . No.

JAMES. I've been out with her on occasion for some time.

TOM. Was that who it was?

JAMES. Yes. Then last week as you were away and we had no ops, well we went out together every night. And well, that's it. Will you be my best man, Tom?

TOM. Sure . . . Have you sort of fixed a date?

JAMES. Complications I'll tell you about, but very soon.

TOM. Fine . . . Congratulations.

JAMES (*after a pause*). Thing is, Tom, I don't know whether I've done right.

TOM. You're not sure about her?

JAMES. No, I'm very sure . . . Thing is if I get the chop . . . She's already lost one bloke.

TOM. Fiancé?

JAMES. No. She was married to a wireless operator in Coastal Command. Disappeared over the Atlantic.

TOM. When?

JAMES. Two years ago. They were only married three months. They'd rented a cottage.

TOM (*after a pause*). She knows the score, James.

JAMES. Yes.

TOM. And she must know you well enough to know that if she had second thoughts —

JAMES. I've said that to her. She's as sure as I am.

TOM. Well then . . . Press on. I'll be proud to be your best man.

JAMES. Thank you, Tom.

TOM. And your old man'll be able to turn out in his kilt and topper.

JAMES. And my mother'll get another new hat.

They both laugh.

TOM. Whizzo. Bang-on.

JAMES. Thing is, Tom, she's older than me.

TOM. How much?

JAMES. Two years. She's 22. Do you think that matters?

TOM. No. I'm a year older than you but I still think of you as a fellow human being, a child of the same God.

JAMES. Decent of you.

TOM. It's just that I've got more flying hours in and I'm that bit wiser and more mature.

JAMES. But shorter.

TOM. What's that got to do with it?

JAMES. Rounding out your analogy. She is too.

They laugh.

JAMES. I'd like you to meet her, Tom.

TOM. I'd like to.

JAMES. I took the liberty of booking a table at the Crown for tomorrow night.

TOM. Fine . . . Except have you seen charts in the met office?

JAMES. No.

TOM. It's possible our services may be required.

Repeat sound of night air battle which opened the play.

Door flung open and closed. TOM *and* JAMES *burst in, weary and fed up.*

TOM. Intelligence officer — he's as thick as a bloody tree trunk.

JAMES (*laughs with derision*). Were we sure it wasn't a dummy airfield we hit?

TOM. I told him there were three 109s taking off.

JAMES. David said two.

TOM. Two or three — what's the bloody odds? The characteristic of dummy aircraft, whatever the number, is that they don't take off. You'd think that'd be apparent even to an intelligence officer.

JAMES. So what's he written it down to?

TOM. I don't know, I came away. His usual one probable, I think. The minimum possible above bugger-all. He thinks he's still a country solicitor filling in bloody income tax returns for farmers. (*He laughs derisively.*) One probable.

JAMES. And that credited to Gale and Hemsdale, no doubt.

TOM. No doubt. He's always round there, a notorious sitter in their armchairs.

JAMES. Complete sycophant.

TOM. Corrupt to the core . . . I'm getting into the sack.

They bounce on to their beds.

JAMES. They still haven't fixed the transfer from my starboard drop tank.

TOM. No.

JAMES. And the instrument dimmer, they put a new thing in — rheostat would it be?

TOM. There's nothing they wouldn't stoop to.

JAMES. It was bad enough before, but now it's either so bright it's like sitting in the middle of Blackpool Illuminations or it's so dark I can't even read the rev counters under my nose. I really will have a go at Alec today.

TOM. He's a dead loss. See Flight Sergeant Whale. Alec's no qualifications.

JAMES. I thought he got a degree in engineering at Aberdeen.

TOM. But in sewage engineering.

JAMES. Surely not.

TOM. Yes, and it's not strictly applicable to his present post except for giving him a very sound working knowledge of how to drop people in the shit.

JAMES. OK for lights out?

TOM. OK.

Click of switch.
Ticking of alarm clock.

TOM (*narration*). We usually came back from operations weary and uncharitable. Flying in combat required a fair amount of brute force — a sort of navvy's job in a sitting posture — and the day leading up to it was often long, attending briefings, doing ground and air tests, and cycling miles between aircraft dispersals and one group of huts and another. Hundreds of people were awheel, endlessly summoned here and there by the loudspeakers. Sometimes, when targets were changed during the day, it would go on for ten hours before take-off, and sometimes at the end the whole thing would be scrubbed when we were strapped in the cockpits, running up the engines. But we had no operation the following night, and I met James' Gwyneth at dinner in the pub. There is nothing much to say about it except that I understood why he wanted to marry her. She was bright but composed and serene, James' counterpart really in a woman, and, sleepy as I was, I could have sat all night in their company.

Strike of cue and click of billiard balls — a cannon.

TOM. Good shot.

Strike of cue. Click of billiard balls.

JAMES. Freddy, this bloke she was married to, he was a very

enterprising sort of bloke. Taught himself the piano and used to pound it out in a miner's club with the pints bouncing on the top.

Strike of cue. Click of billiard balls.

TOM. Was he a coal miner?

JAMES. Yes. He only volunteered for aircrew to get out of the mines.

TOM. What did he fly in?

JAMES. Sunderlands. He did the cooking and apparently became very good at it. Genned himself up from a book and did 'em very delicate repasts.

TOM. Must be funny flying a kite big enough to cook in.

JAMES. You'd get used to it. I believe taxi-ing's dicey, though, in a flying boat because you've got the current to cope with as well as the wind.

Strike of cue. Click of balls. One drops into pocket.

She'd been quite nervous at the prospect of meeting you.

TOM (*surprised*). Nervous — of me?

JAMES. You alarm people.

TOM. I alarm people?

JAMES. They don't know when you're joking.

TOM. I don't know myself.

JAMES. And you've a very decisive manner, you know.

TOM. I cultivate that.

JAMES. I know.

TOM. I don't overheat my cylinder head with ratiocination.

JAMES. That's apparent.

TOM. I work on the excellent naval principle, 'Say something, if only goodbye.'

JAMES. I know, but other people don't — which is why you alarm them. (*He laughs.*)

Strike of cue. Click of balls — a cannon.

Shot . . . When we're married, Gwyneth and me, do you think they'll post one of us away?

TOM. Not deliberately I don't suppose as an act of policy but if a posting came up — ask old Harry.

Strike of cue. Click of balls — a cannon.

JAMES. If I did get permission to live out or whatever's necessary, I trust you wouldn't be offended, Tom.

TOM. Christ, no.

JAMES. Just thought I'd mention —

TOM. Provided, of course, I don't get some scrofulous warrior in your pit.

JAMES. You've a right to a room to yourself.

TOM. I like a room-mate. I'll have him deloused as a precaution.

JAMES. And you'd be all right with the stove?

TOM. Sure.

Silence.

(*Kindly*:) James, what's on your mind?

JAMES. Well, a sort of legal thing.

TOM. Legal thing?

JAMES. Whether Freddy's dead for legal purposes. You know, whether she's free to remarry. He was posted missing, well how long after that does it take for people to be presumed killed?

TOM. Six months, isn't it?

JAMES. It can't be, surely. Blokes have come back through Spain and Sweden after two years.

TOM. He can't come back through anywhere, James. They were lost over the North Atlantic, weren't they?

JAMES. Yes.

TOM. They went into the drink then. There's nowhere else for them to go. Was anything sighted — wreckage, oil?

JAMES. Nothing.

TOM. That's it then. They wouldn't last three minutes in the North Atlantic in winter. Old Harry'll know all about the legal aspects. Ask him.

JAMES. She said she'd prefer to inquire herself.

TOM. Fair enough.

JAMES. It *was* winter when he went missing — February and nothing but snowdrops in the garden of this cottage they rented. He got hanging baskets of flowers from somewhere and hung them round the house.

TOM (*after a pause*). Did he? . . . I see.

Cue strikes ball. Balls crash, bounce hard from cush and crash again.

TOM (*narration*). Freddy became, if you count the stove, an honorary fourth member of our abode. James often came back from seeing Gwyneth with some story about him, and even to me at third hand this man, long dead and never known to either of us, assumed a quite vivid existence. One weekend James went to London with Gwyneth and he came back not only with further information about Freddy but also with another volume of Proust, which Gwyneth had discovered for me in a second-hand bookshop.

JAMES. She made the point that she didn't wish to take up all my time.

TOM. Sure.

JAMES. You know, that you and I should slope off together sometimes.

TOM. We have bags of time. I don't like London.

JAMES. She just didn't want you to feel —

TOM. I don't, James. Not in the least . . . *'Time Regained'*.

JAMES. The final volume. The only one she could find.

TOM. It's very good of her.

JAMES. And I know you're not troubling about the order you read them in.

TOM. I'll use this to shame old Harry. I'll point out that it's a gift and I can't get stuck into it until he remembers the volumes he keeps forgetting to knock off from West Croxford.

JAMES. You could maybe take a wee dip into it like people sneak a look at the end of detective tales.

TOM. No, I'll keep it and treasure it, then apart from these two I've read, I can go through the whole shoot in the correct firing order..

JAMES (*laughs*). It might actually be an advantage to have just the last one.

TOM. How?

JAMES. If you had to plough through the whole lot and got the chop in the middle you'd never know how it ends. This way you can go down laughing.

TOM. Thanks. I'll give you a resumé, so if similarly placed, you'll be in a position to join in the mirth.

JAMES (*laughs, then factually*). We slept together.

TOM. How did you cope?

JAMES. OK. She'd had previous experience, of course, got a few hours in.

TOM. Enjoyable?

JAMES. Fine.

TOM. It's something I keep meaning to try myself.

JAMES. I can recommend it. Bang-on.

TOM. Has she managed to sort out the legalities about Freddy?

JAMES. Yes. She can go ahead and marry . . . But she asked me not to press her, give her time.

TOM. When was this?

JAMES. Coming back in the train . . . She's always believed he'd return.

TOM (*gently*). That's not possible.

JAMES. She knows. But she's continued to visit his family in Yorkshire and it's sort of left implicit between them that he might come back, though probably only his mother really believes it any more.

TOM. I understand.

JAMES. But it's become a sort of faith with Gwyneth as well, you know, not reason but like people have religious faith . . . She prays for him.

TOM. I see.

JAMES (*after a pause*). She'd never been out with anybody until me and she thought that sleeping with me might just finally — (*He stops, unable to find words.*)

TOM (*gently*). Transfer poor old Fred to the right filing cabinet?

JAMES. Yes.

TOM. It could hardly be expected — just overnight.

JAMES. I know, that's why she said, give her a little more time.

TOM (*narration*). Gwyneth, who had waited so long for Freddy, was constant also in her waiting for James. When he was due back from an operational flight she came to the edge of the woods by the perimeter track like an early-morning animal and waited until he taxied into his dispersal, then quietly went. She waited on the morning when all the crews got back except James with Bill Slater and left their aircraft standing silent round the field. Trees dripped, the runway lights sparkled in the mist and she waited, trim and compact, as though she were standing at a bus stop, globules of moisture forming a grey down over the wool of her greatcoat as the minutes went by . . . He arrived silently, a flat bird hanging against the mist, undercarriage descending, port engine stopped, wing tattered, fuselage streaked with oil. He touched down, throwing up spray, losing speed nicely, across the intersection, slowing, rolling, almost stopped, turning off with a burst from the good engine.

Firemen, fast out on their tender, threatened the aircraft with nozzles like asbestos pistoleros, and medical orderlies wormed in through the hatch in the fuselage. They were a long time inside, and they brought out Bill Slater dead and slotted his stretcher into their ambulance, like a baker's tray into a bread van, and drove away. James crossed the grass head down, a batsman returning to the pavilion after a lost innings, walking slowly to postpone the ordeal of a sympathetic reception. The episode helped Gwyneth to a decision.

JAMES. She's going to see Freddy's folks.

TOM. Yes.

JAMES. Tell 'em herself.

TOM. Sure.

JAMES. Then we'll bang in for a few days' leave. See her folks and mine.

TOM. Sure.

Silence.

JAMES. Her old man has a grocer's shop near Caernarvon.

TOM. An honourable calling.

JAMES (*with some bitterness*). If he's looking for an errand lad I might not come back.

TOM. Sure.

JAMES. I'd settle for that, doing deliveries for her old man.

TOM. It's a start.

JAMES. And only a start. I'd have a whole lifetime with her and finish up a retired grocer.

TOM. It's a fair pinnacle.

JAMES. That won't be reached by most of our friends.

TOM. No.

JAMES. Nor by the poor sods we've sent down in flames. Nor by millions of people on both sides who've died in torment and millions more to come.

TOM. No.

Silence.

JAMES. If I didn't have Gwyneth, Tom, I don't think I could go on.

TOM. No.

JAMES. It's, you know, my confidence.

TOM. Anybody'd be shaken.

JAMES. I don't mean just now. For weeks past.

TOM. It doesn't show.

JAMES. No . . . I *can* hold on, Tom. She's gone through a bad time but you'd never guess, would you?

TOM. You certainly wouldn't.

JAMES. She has this kind of serenity . . . It just helps, that's all.

TOM. Sure.

JAMES (*after a pause*). I didn't know he was dead till they lifted him out of the kite.

TOM (*narration*). There was a very good walk from the airfield. You saw men working in the fields behind great horses, and the air was sweet with the smell of nettlegrown farmyards. We were never beyond the sound of aero-engines but it was a noise we didn't hear. From the top of a rise on a clear day we could count twelve church towers and watch a panting engine haul its toy wagons slowly across the plain. James led me out on this stroll the day after Gwyneth got back from seeing Freddy's folks.

A little birdsong, some distant country sounds which persist through the scene.

JAMES. His old lady wept, but his old man and his brother told her to go ahead. His brother took her down to the club for a few pints and kind of said, 'You see, they've got a new pianist' and he introduced another bloke and said 'This gentleman's taken over Freddy's share of the whippets and I've taken over Freddy's suits'.

TOM. *slight laugh.*

Apparently it all ended with jokes about him needing to let out the waist and backside, and some old wives discovered what it was all about and they all proceeded to a booze-up in honour of Gwyneth's forthcoming marriage.

TOM. Great people.

JAMES. Apparently his father said 'It's the sensible thing, Gwyneth. Mother knows he's gone, but write to her if you would for a time.'

TOM. Sort of moving, isn't it?

JAMES. Yes.

TOM. So it's all OK?

JAMES. It's all OK.

TOM. I'm very pleased, James, very pleased.

JAMES. Just get a week's leave now and see her folks and mine.

TOM. Bang-on.

They both laugh with pleasure.

You were down at the flights this morning.

JAMES (*embarrassed*). Yes.

TOM. Taking counsel with Alec and Flight Sergeant Whale.

JAMES laughs with embarrassment.

In most earnest conclave.

JAMES. I was hoping you wouldn't know.

TOM. Are you going to tell me or shall I guess?

JAMES. Don't guess. You'll guess right.

TOM. Unpredictable feed from the drop tank to the starboard outer?

JAMES laughs with embarrassment.

And what other neuroses did you divine in your brief flight in this new and apparently excellent aircraft?

JAMES (*laughs*). Not a neurosis, it's a fault. You try it.

TOM. An additional fault?

JAMES. Yes. Engines splutter when she's bounced hard.

TOM. Cough.

JAMES. More than a cough.

TOM. They all do. They don't like negative g.

JAMES. It's more than that. There's a carburation fault.

TOM. What did the plumbers say?

JAMES. Alec recited his piece from the textbook and Flight Sergeant Whale said he'd check through. Obviously they thought what you think.

They both laugh.

TOM. I was thinking of awarding you a clock as a wedding present.

JAMES. We could use a clock fine.

TOM. It'd develop hypochondria. It'll have to be something non-mechanical — a pair of book ends perhaps.

JAMES. Fine. We mean to do a bit of reading.

They both laugh. A silence between them, in which country sounds are heard.

You know what I said about feeling good.

TOM. When last mentioned it was about not feeling bad.

JAMES. Same thing. She said I gave her confidence the same way.

TOM. You can see she feels good.

JAMES. She said she was very happy with Freddy, but he was a good bit older, and his kind of sparkling personality, she sort of felt — not quite dominated.

TOM. Subdued?

JAMES. Not even as strong as that. Overshadowed a wee bit.

TOM. Yes.

JAMES (*after a pause*). She said she'd never said that to anybody before.

TOM (*narration*). James and Gwyneth got their leave and went off to see their parents and arrange a wedding date. Good weather blessed their trip and gave the squadron an excellent week. We flew three operations, two sticking round the bomber stream at 20,000 feet and one a low-level attack on airfields. I was sorry James missed it. He came back a day earlier than expected and was flaked out on top of his bed when I got in quite late in the evening.

TOM (*surprised*). James!

JAMES (*pleased*). Tom.

TOM. Good to see you.

JAMES. Good to see you.

They laugh with pleasure.

TOM. Back early.

JAMES (*tinge of tiredness in his voice*). Train times.

TOM. Is something amiss, James?

JAMES (*uncertainly*). No . . . No.

TOM. I've been wielding the cue down at the mess. Why didn't you come down?

JAMES. I did. I observed you wielding the cue . . . Didn't want to disturb you.

TOM. Oh, for Christ's sake!

JAMES. They tell me the squadron shot down seven.

TOM. George actually credited us with seven in his intelligence reports.

JAMES. And two to you personally.

TOM. George's sanity waxes and wanes with the phases of the moon. He's going through a sound phase.

JAMES. What were they?

TOM. A 110 that was throttling back in a leisurely way for a position under a Lancaster and a Ju88 that we had a bit of a dice round with first. Cyril Gale claimed an He-219A.

JAMES. Rare kite.

TOM. Rare bloke.

They laugh.

We got nothing credited for the low-level job but that's fair enough.

JAMES. You can't offer an inventory.

TOM. Some bloody great explosions though. They couldn't all have been NAAFI tea vans.

JAMES. Did George say they were?

TOM. Not this time, but he's said it before, hasn't he?

JAMES. Oh yes.

TOM. When he's been cavorting through his maniac phase.

JAMES *laughs a little and slightly awkwardly.*

Silence. TOM *waits to hear* JAMES' *news, then resumes, making conversation.*

Old Harry got a letter back from Bill Slater's dad.

JAMES. I meant to go and see Bill's dad.

TOM. He's keeping his letter for you to see.

JAMES. I'd have gone to see him except things took up more time than − (*He peters out.*)

TOM. Yes . . . Sure.

JAMES (*after a pause*). I'll go next week.

TOM. Sure.

Silence.

JAMES. It hasn't worked out, Tom.

TOM (*gently*). Your arrangements?

JAMES. Yes . . . We visited my folks first, which was what Gwyneth wanted, and it went really well there. They'd obviously had forebodings, but as soon as they met her, Tom −

TOM. I can well imagine.

JAMES. My mother, I've never seen her so pleased. She said, 'You marry her. You will not find another like that one.' . . . The old man forked out for a dinner at the Caledonian Hotel. Then we went down to her home and I don't want to put it wrong, Tom, her folks were fine and friendly but it kind of got dragged out.

TOM. Weighing you up?

JAMES. No. That's the galling thing about it. There was no question of opposition. Most welcoming. It all began to founder on detail.

TOM. Detail?

JAMES. Arrangements. I told you her old man belonged to a particular religious sect.

TOM. Sort of fanatic.

JAMES. No. No. It isn't at all a fanatical sect, but being Welsh they don't have many chapels outside Wales.

TOM. Fair enough.

JAMES. He wanted us to marry in their local chapel, which is where she married Freddy and I'd have gone along with that but Gwyneth wouldn't because she wanted it here where our friends are. I know she was thinking mainly of me. She knows they won't take the blokes off the order of battle for a couple of days to attend a wedding.

TOM. Surely the blokes aren't so important.

JAMES. I wasn't in on the argument, Tom. Gwyneth talked to her father in a different room and her mother would sail in and out and say something cheerful to me about the weather and maybe brew up. Apparently, there was a sort of compromise between them and we all trotted down to see the minister to get him to look up whether there was a chapel of the right sort round here. He gave us a letter for a minister at Kings Lynn.

TOM. That's handy enough.

JAMES. Yes . . . Then we trotted round visiting her relations, which was fair enough, except she was on edge, Tom, you know, shaken.

TOM. You don't know what else her father might have said in this long conversation.

JAMES. No, I don't . . . It wasn't her father, Tom, at least not for what mattered.

TOM (*after a pause*). I see.

JAMES (*after a pause*). We stayed on the way back at a hotel near Chester. She couldn't sleep, so we stuck the light on.

TOM. Yes.

JAMES (*after a pause*). You know that when Freddy went missing she wouldn't allow herself to accept he was dead. She felt her faith and will might somehow — it's not a hundred per cent superstition, Tom. When I was struggling back the other morning I knew you willed me back, Tom. It helped.

TOM (*gently*). But it didn't bring poor old Bill Slater back from the dead, James.

JAMES. No . . . As time passed she didn't really believe Freddy would come back. Then his dad started to spin stories about him pitching up in Greenland and living in igloos with Esquimos so she knew pretty early he'd given him up.

TOM. And, as you told me, on her last visit the whole of Freddy's family made it absolutely clear they'd given him up.

JAMES. So have hers, and that's what led to this — complication.

TOM. Complication?

JAMES. Yes. When we were trotting round her relatives we went to an aunt who had tactfully removed Freddy's photograph from the mantelpiece . . . It just finally brought it home to her that every-body had given him up.

TOM (*meaning why not?*). Yes.

JAMES (*after a pause*). You know she's a believer, Tom.

TOM. Yes.

JAMES. Well, she prayed every night for his safe return, and she acted in faith. She never went out with anybody until me.

TOM. You said.

JAMES. Well, apparently in recent weeks she's kept the prayers just about going.

TOM. Tick-over revs.

JAMES (*short laugh*). Tick-over revs. And the fact that Freddy's family wrote him off didn't affect the issue because they're not praying people. But her family are. And when she saw his picture gone from her aunt's mantelpiece it brought it home that her family had ceased to pray for him.

TOM. Yes.

JAMES. And that there was only her left to pray, exactly because of the intentions she'd conveyed to people.

TOM. Sure.

JAMES. And that if she now ceased to pray it was kind of cancelling a request to God.

TOM. In effect saying 'scrub it'.

JAMES. Yes. Conveying that it was OK now for Him to withdraw his protection from poor old Freddy, dump him.

TOM. James, this is theology and I'm lost. But we do know that, prayers or no prayers, poor old Freddy and his many accomplishments was a block of ice five minutes after he hit the ocean.

JAMES. She knows, and she said it's not even a proper prayer to persist in, obstinately asking God to change his will. But it remains an act of faith, perverse though she knows it to be, a kind of last strand of fidelity.

TOM. It seems sort of theoretical.

JAMES. But not to her and it didn't seem theoretical to me last night seeing her trying to explain it, sitting up in bed with the light on.

TOM. She was tired.

JAMES: *Weary.* It might never have happened if she hadn't been upset with all the argy-bargy and trotting round seeing relatives and the minister. But it's as well it did. It sort of made things clear that might not otherwise − (*He peters out.*)

TOM (*not understanding*). I see.

JAMES. She said she hadn't been fair to me. She said she thought she was using me.

TOM. Using you?

JAMES. She said as a substitute, but then she said that wasn't really what she meant. She said she should have got spiritually free from Freddy before she met me.

TOM. That wasn't her fault. You sought her out.

JAMES. She said she knew I was right for her. Freddy dazzled her. She said she knew now she'd never seen the promise of a whole lifetime in him, and she thought, especially after the visit to his folks, that in time he'd just pass into the bygone.

TOM. Which he would have done, which he had done. It was just a final flare-up brought on by the circumstances.

JAMES. I failed her. When she said yes to me she was depending on me gently and finally to wipe Freddy off the slate. But I didn't even know I had that to do.

TOM. How could you know?

JAMES. If I'd have been anything, Tom, but a bloody nonentity I wouldn't have needed to know. It would simply have happened.

TOM. You're not a nonentity, by Christ you're not. She didn't want a load of bloody antics. She wanted you because you're steadfast enough for a lifetime. She said that, didn't she?

JAMES. Something like that. She said it several times.

TOM (*pause, then gently*). So what's going to happen, James?

JAMES. Nothing.

TOM. Nothing?

JAMES. It's scrubbed.

TOM. When was that decided?

JAMES. This morning when daylight came up . . . I think I'll get into the sack, Tom. (*He tries to laugh.*) Seems a long time since my last proper sleep at her parents' place.

TOM. Sure.

Sound of JAMES *winding the alarm clock.*

TOM (*tentatively*). James . . . If I may just put a thought.

JAMES. Surely, Tom.

TOM. It doesn't have to be immediate, does it? If you give it a bit of time, Freddy must fade away now. These curious events may actually be helpful. It may well be they've tossed Freddy up to the surface for his final appearance . . . Hang on a bit, then don't bugger about with chapels and all sorts of religious complications. Just nip in and see the padre and get it done at the double on the firm.

JAMES. We did discuss something of the sort. I think she would have been willing.

TOM. But you weren't?

JAMES. No. Things became clear for me that I should have realised from the beginning. As you said, Tom, she wants me for a lifetime, and I don't have a lifetime to give. Another three-month marriage —

TOM. Balls.

JAMES. All right. Six months, a year. Knowing how it's hurt her, I can't ask her to go through it again. What like a life would that leave her with?

TOM. You're not going to get the chop.

JAMES. I shalln't see the end of this war.

TOM. You better had. You get yourself killed and I'll have you shot.

JAMES (*laughs a little, then finally*). So that's it.

Silence.

TOM. I'm sorry, James. I'm very sad for both of you.

JAMES. Yes . . . OK for lights out?

TOM. OK.

Click of light switch.
Creak of bed springs.

JAMES. She's going to put in for a posting in the morning.

TOM. Yes.

JAMES. And maybe if I'm still around when the war ends, maybe — (*He peters out.*)

TOM. Sure. (*Trying to cheer him and uncertainly:*) Since you are back, James —

JAMES. Yes.

TOM. There's something you might like to do tomorrow . . . Shall I save it?

JAMES. Tell me.

TOM. Old Harry wanted to see you as soon as you got back.

JAMES. Fine.

TOM. I think it's about your gong.

JAMES. Fine.

TOM. In fact, I know it's about your gong.

JAMES. Grand.

TOM. But don't say you know. Old Harry wanted to be the first to tell you.

JAMES. Sure.

Silence. Alarm clock ticks.

TOM. What I thought, James, sort of leaping ahead, I thought we might celebrate it with a dinner party in London. I don't know whether that would sort of seem — (*He peters out.*)

JAMES. It'd be fine . . . I'd like that.

TOM. Invite your mother and your old man and the blokes if they're stood down, and Alec, Old Harry if he'd come . . .

JAMES (*laughs a little*). He won't. He repairs days off to a county lady with a baronial hall.

TOM. Bring his baronial lady. Everybody come. You know, real big do. I've got £45.

JAMES. You're very kind, Tom.

TOM. Then afterwards we'll whip back here and top up the topers at the bar.

JAMES (*laughs a little*). Bang-on.

Silence. Ticking of clock.

TOM (*tentatively*). There's something I've really been looking forward to telling you — if you're not too tired.

JAMES. I'd like to hear.

TOM. Catastrophe has befallen Gale and Hemsdale.

JAMES. Pranged?

TOM. Better than that. One of their personal armchairs has been written off.

JAMES (*laughs, for the first time easily*). How did that happen?

TOM. Usual rough house their soirées develop into. Collapsed under a heap of scuffling ruffians, legs splayed out, springs sticking up, absolutely wrecked.

JAMES (*laughs*). Whizzo.

TOM. And the handle got knocked off their jerry.

JAMES *laughs.*

so it's no longer decently portable when full. They've planted bulbs in it.

JAMES *laughs.*

Yep. Which Alec says won't prosper because of the extremes of temperature caused by their self-vandalised stove.

JAMES (*laughs*). They really have hit rock bottom.

TOM. Absolutely. They've taken to drinking meths.

JAMES *laughs.*

And our good and faithful servant, the arsonist Lusty, is almost permanently absent conducting a wholesale greengrocery business round the farms.

JAMES. How does he manage to get away with that?

TOM. You ask him. He doesn't talk to me.

JAMES *laughs.*

Oh, and the best thing of all I nearly forgot to tell you. The Station Commander's landed in deep dirt.

JAMES (*delighted*). The Station Commander.

TOM. Up to the neck. He's been burying kitchen waste instead of sending it to a depot of the Ministry of Agriculture, contrary to God knows how many orders.

JAMES. Mutiny.

TOM. Yep. He's up for a drum-head court martial with every prospect that he'll be shot.

JAMES. Bang-on. I've obviously missed a very crowded week.

TOM. There'll be others . . . The new Canadian-built aircraft O for Oboe that you flew briefly before your leave.

JAMES. Yes.

TOM. It's actually a replacement not for the kite you wrote off but for the one Tim Unwin got clobbered in.

JAMES. I know.

TOM. But it's agreed you can consider it yours for the time being, subject you know to the usual maintenance turnover.

JAMES. That's great. It's a fine kite — just minor snags, as mentioned.

TOM. I'm coming to that. I flew it on two of last week's operations and I reckon it has fifteen knots over anything on the squadron.

JAMES. The engines seemed really good.

TOM. And aerodynamically. Alec's mob haven't had time yet to scuff up the leading edges with their ladders.

JAMES. Were you flying it when you bagged the two?

TOM. As it happens, no. But it was very sweet indeed in ground attack, just that extra tautness, beautiful.

JAMES. It smelled new. The Canadian ones smell different.

TOM. Yes . . . And those snags you were complaining of . . . .

JAMES *laughs a little with some self-consciousness.*

You were quite right. They were faults. Even I could detect 'em.

JAMES *slight laugh.*

And they've been fixed.

JAMES. Fine . . . Well, fine.

TOM. The carburation — Flight Sergeant Whale will tell you what they found.

JAMES. I'd like to know for interest.

TOM. The transfer from the starboard drop tank, Alec offered a lot of flannel but I don't honestly think they know what they've done.

JAMES *slight laugh.*

Just pulled it to bits and blew through some pipes and put it together again.

JAMES *slight laugh.*

TOM. But it's OK now.

JAMES. Grand.

TOM. Absolutely spot on.

JAMES. Fine.

TOM. Perfection. You'll be laughing.

JAMES. Bang on.

Ticking of alarm clock.

Cross fade to:
Sound of night air battle used at beginning of the play.

FAMILY VOICES

by Harold Pinter

Harold Pinter was born in London in 1930. He wrote his first play, *The Room,* in 1957 while he was an actor in repertory, and completed *The Dumb Waiter* and *The Birthday Party* during the same year. Since then he has produced a body of work for the stage, television and films which has given him an international reputation. In 1960 *The Caretaker,* his first big success, received both the Evening Standard Drama Award for the best play of the year and the Page 1 Award of the Newspaper Guild of New York. In 1967 *The Homecoming* won the Drama Critics' Circle Award on Broadway. *Old Times* (Royal Shakespeare Company, 1971) was followed by two plays for the National Theatre, *No Man's Land* (1975) and *Betrayal* (1978). *The Hothouse,* written in 1958, had its first production at the Hampstead Theatre, London in 1980.

Family Voices was first broadcast on BBC Radio 3 on 22nd January 1981. The cast was as follows:

VOICE 1, *a young man*   Michael Kitchen
VOICE 2, *a woman*   Peggy Ashcroft
VOICE 3, *a man*   Mark Dignam

Director: Peter Hall

Family Voices was subsequently presented in a 'platform performance' by the National Theatre, London, on 13th February 1981. Cast and director were the same. The decor was by John Bury.

VOICE 1. I am having a very nice time.

The weather is up and down, but surprisingly warm, on the whole, more often than not.

I hope you're feeling well, and not as peaky as you did, the last time I saw you.

No, you didn't feel peaky, you felt perfectly well, you simply looked peaky.

Do you miss me?

I am having a very nice time and I hope you are glad of that.

At the moment I am dead drunk.

I had five pints in The Fishmongers Arms tonight, followed by three double scotches, and literally rolled home.

When I say home I can assure you that my room is extremely pleasant. So is the bathroom. Extremely pleasant. I have some very pleasant baths indeed in the bathroom. So does everybody else in the house. They all lie quite naked in the bath and have very pleasant baths indeed. All the people in the house go about saying what a superb bath and bathroom the one we share is, they go about telling literally everyone they meet what lovely baths you can get in this place, more or less unparalleled, to put it bluntly.

It's got a lot to do with the landlady, who is a Mrs Withers, a person who turns out to be an utterly charming person of impeccable credentials.

When I said I was drunk I was of course making a joke.

I bet you laughed.

Mother?

Did you get the joke? You know I never touch alcohol.

I like being in this enormous city, all by myself. I expect to make friends in the not too distant future.

I expect to make girlfriends too.

I expect to meet a very nice girl. Having met her, I shall bring her home to meet my mother.

I like walking in this enormous city, all by myself. It's fun to know no-one at all. When I pass people in the street they don't realise that I don't know them from Adam. They know other people and even more other people know them, so they naturally think that even if I don't know them I know the other people. So they look at me, they try to catch my eye, they expect me to speak. But as I do not know them I do not speak. Nor do I ever feel the slightest temptation to do so.

You see, mother, I am not lonely, because all that has ever happened to me is with me, keeps me company; my childhood, for example, through which you, my mother, and he, my father, guided me.

I get on very well with my landlady, Mrs Withers. She tells me I am her solace. I have a drink with her at lunchtime and another one at teatime and then take her for a couple in the evening at The Fishmongers Arms.

She was in the Women's Air Force in the Second World War. Don't drop a bollock, Charlie, she's fond of saying, Call him Flight Sergeant and he'll be as happy as a pig in shit.

You'd really like her, mother.

I think it's dawn. I can see it coming up. Another day. A day I warmly welcome. And so I shall end this letter to you, my dear mother, with my love.

VOICE 2. Darling. Where are you? The flowers are wonderful here. The blooms. You so loved them. Why do you never write?

I think of you and wonder how you are. Do you ever think of me? Your mother? Ever? At all?

Have you changed your address?

Have you made friends with anyone? A nice boy? Or a nice girl?

There are so many nice boys and girls about. But please don't get mixed up with the other sort. They can land you in such terrible trouble. And you'd hate it so. You're so scrupulous, so particular.

I often think that I would love to live happily ever after with you and your young wife. And she would be such a lovely wife to you and I would have the occasional dinner with you both. A dinner I would be quite happy to cook myself, should you both be tired after your long day, as I'm sure you will be.

I sometimes walk the cliff path and think of you. I think of the times you walked the cliff path, with your father, with cheese sandwiches. Didn't you? You both sat on the clifftop and ate my cheese sandwiches together. Do you remember our little joke? Munch, munch. We had a damn good walk, your father would say. You mean you had a good munch munch, I would say. And you would both laugh.

Darling. I miss you. I gave birth to you. Where are you?

I wrote to you three months ago, telling you of your father's death. Did you receive my letter?

VOICE 1. I'm not at all sure that I like the people in this house, apart from Mrs Withers and her daughter, Jane. Jane is a schoolgirl who works hard at her homework.

She keeps her nose to the grindstone. This I find impressive. There's not too much of that about these days. But I'm not so sure about the other people in this house.

One is an old man.

The one who is an old man retires early. He is bald.

The other is a woman who wears red dresses.

The other one is another man.

He is big. He is much bigger than the other man. His hair is black. He has black eyebrows and black hair on the back of his hands.

I ask Mrs Withers about them but she will talk of nothing but her days in the Women's Air Force in the Second World War.

I have decided that Jane is not Mrs Wither's daughter but her grand-daughter. Mrs Withers is seventy. Jane is fifteen. That I am convinced is the truth.

At night I hear whispering from the other rooms and do not understand it. I hear steps on the stairs but do not dare go out to investigate.

VOICE 2. As your father grew closer to his death he spoke more and more of you, with tenderness and bewilderment. I consoled him with the idea that you had left home to make him proud of you. I think I succeeded in this. One of his last sentences was: Give him a slap on the back from me. Give him a slap on the back from me.

VOICE 1. I have made a remarkable discovery. The old man who is bald and who retires early is named Withers. Benjamin Withers. Unless it is simply a coincidence it must mean that he is a relation.

I asked Mrs Withers what the truth of this was. She poured herself a gin and looked at it before she drank it. Then she looked at me and said: You are my little pet. I've always wanted a little pet but I've never had one and now I've got one.

Sometimes she gives me a cuddle, as if she were my mother.

But I haven't forgotten that I have a mother and that you are my mother.

VOICE 2. Sometimes I wonder if you remember that you have a mother.

VOICE 1. Something has happened. The woman who wears red dresses stopped me and asked me into her room for a cup of tea. I went into her room. It was far bigger than I had expected, with sofas and curtains and veils and shrouds and rugs and soft material all over the walls, dark blue. Jane was sitting on a sofa doing her homework, by the look of it. I was invited to sit on the same sofa. Tea had already been made and stood ready, in a china teaset, of a most elegant design. I was given a cup. So was Jane, who smiled at me. I haven't introduced myself, the woman said, my name is Lady Withers. Jane sipped her tea with her legs up on the sofa. Her stockinged toes came to rest on my thigh. It wasn't the biggest sofa in the world. Lady Withers sat opposite us on a substantially bigger sofa. Her dress, I decided, wasn't red but pink. Jane was in green, apart from her toes, which were clad in black. Lady Withers asked me about you, mother. She asked me about my mother. I said, with absolute conviction, that you were the best mother in the world. She asked me to call her Lally. And to call Jane Jane. I said I did call Jane Jane. Jane gave me a bun. I think it was a bun. Lady Withers bit into her bun. Jane bit into her bun, her toes now resting on my lap. Lady Withers seemed to be enjoying her bun, on her sofa. She finished it and picked up another. I had never seen so many buns. One quick glance told me they were perched on cakestands all over the room. Lady Withers went through her second bun with no trouble at all and was at once on to another. Jane, on the other hand, chewed almost dreamily at her bun and when a currant was left stranded on her upper lip she licked it off, without haste. I could not reconcile this with the fact that her toes were quite restless, even agitated. Her mouth, eating, was measured, serene; her toes, not eating, were agitated, highly strung, some would say hysterical. My bun turned out to be rock solid. I bit into it, it jumped out of my mouth and bounced into my lap. Jane's feet caught it. It calmed her toes down. She juggled the bun, with some expertise, along them. I recalled that, in an early exchange between us, she had told me she wanted to be an acrobat.

VOICE 2. Darling. Where are you? Why do you never write? Nobody knows your whereabouts. Nobody knows if you are alive or dead. Nobody can find you. Have you changed your name?

If you are alive you are a monster. On his deathbed your father cursed you. He cursed me too, to tell the truth. He cursed everyone in sight. Except that you were not in sight. I do not blame you entirely for your father's ill humour, but your absence and silence were a great burden on him, a weariness to him. He died in lamentation and oath. Was that your wish? Now I am alone, apart from Millie, who sometimes comes over from Dover. She is some consolation. Her eyes well with tears when she speaks of you, your dear sister's eyes well with tears. She has made a truly happy marriage and has a lovely little boy. When he is older he will want to know where his uncle is. What shall we say?

Or perhaps you will arrive here in a handsome new car, one day, in the not too distant future, in a nice new suit, quite out of the blue, and hold me in your arms.

VOICE 1. Lady Withers stood up. As Jane is doing her homework, she said, perhaps you would care to leave and come again another day. Jane withdrew her feet, my bun clasped between her two big toes. Yes of course, I said, unless Jane would like me to help her with her homework. No thank you, said Lady Withers, I shall help her with her homework.

What I didn't say is that I am thinking of offering myself out as a tutor. I consider that I would make an excellent tutor, to the young, in any one of a number of subjects. Jane would be an ideal pupil. She possesses a true love of learning. That is the sense of her one takes from her every breath, her every sigh and exhalation. When she turns her eyes upon you, you see within her eyes, raw, untutored, unexercised but willing, a deep love of learning.

These are midnight thoughts, mother, although the time is ten twenty-three, precisely.

VOICE 2. Darling?

VOICE 1. While I was lying in my bath this afternoon, thinking on these things, there was apparently a knock on the front door. The man with black hair apparently opened the door. Two women stood on the doorstep. They said they were my mother and my sister, and asked for me. He denied knowledge of me. No, he had not heard of me. No, there was no-one of that name resident. This was a family house, no strangers admitted. No, they got on very well, thank you very much, without intruders. I suggest, he said, that you both go back to where you come from, and stop bothering innocent hardworking people with your slanders and your libels, these all too predictable excrescences of the depraved mind at the end of its tether. I can smell your sort a mile off and I am quite prepared to put you both on a charge of malicious mischief, insulting behaviour and vagabondage, in other words wandering around on doorsteps knowingly, without any visible means of support. So piss off out of it before I call a copper.

I was lying in my bath when the door opened. I thought I had locked it. My name's Riley, he said, how's the bath? Very nice, I said. You've got a wellknit yet slender frame, he said, I thought you only a snip, I never imagined you would be as wellknit and slender as I now see you are. Oh thank you, I said. Don't thank me, he said, It's God you have to thank. Or your mother. I've just dismissed a couple of imposters at the front door. We'll get no more shit from that quarter. He then sat on the edge of the bath and recounted to me what I've just recounted to you.

It interests me that my father wasn't bothered to make the trip.

VOICE 2. I hear your father's step on the stair. I hear his cough. But his step and his cough fade. He does not open the door.

Sometimes I think I have always been sitting like this. I sometimes think I have always been sitting like this, alone by an indifferent fire, curtains closed, night, winter.

You see, I have my thoughts too. Thoughts no-one else knows I have, thoughts none of my family ever knew I had. But I write of them to you now, wherever you are.

What I mean is that when, for example, I was washing your hair, with the most delicate shampoo, and rinsing, and then drying your hair so gently with my soft towel, so that no murmur came from you, of discomfort or unease, and then looked into your eyes, and saw you look into mine, knowing that you wanted no-one else, no-one at all, knowing that you were entirely happy in my arms, I knew also, for example, that I was at the same time sitting by an indifferent fire, alone in winter, in eternal night without you.

VOICE 1. Lady Withers plays the piano. They were sitting, the three women, about the room. About the room were bottles of a vin rosé, of a pink I shall never forget. They sipped their wine from such lovely glass, an elegance of gesture and grace I thought long dead. Lady Withers wore a necklace around her alabaster neck, a neck amazingly young. She played Schumann. She smiled at me. Mrs Withers and Jane smiled at me. I took a seat. I took it and sat in it. I will never leave it.

Oh mother, I have found my home, my family. Little did I ever dream I could know such happiness.

VOICE 2. Perhaps I should forget all about you. Perhaps I should curse you as your father cursed you. Oh I pray, I pray your life is a torment to you. I wait for your letter begging me to come to you. I'll spit on it.

VOICE 1. Mother, mother, I've had the most unpleasant, the most mystifying encounter, with the man who calls himself Mr Withers. Will you give me your advice?

Come in here, son, he called. Look sharp. Don't mess about. I haven't got all night. I went in. A jug. A basin. A bicycle.

You know where you are? he said. You're in my room. It's not Euston station. Get me? It's a true oasis.

This is the only room in this house where you can pick up a
caravanserai to all points West. Compris? Comprende? Get me? Are
you prepared to follow me down the mountain? Look at me. My
name's Withers. I'm there or thereabouts. Follow? Embargo on all
duff terminology. With me? Embargo on all things redundant.
All areas in that connection verboten. You're in a diseaseridden
land, boxer. Keep your weight on all the left feet you can lay your
hands on. Keep dancing. The old foxtrot is the classical response but
that's not the response I'm talking about. Nor am I talking
about the other response. Up the slaves. Get me? This is a place of
creatures, up and down stairs. Creatures of the rhythmic splits, the
rhythmic sideswipes, the rums and roulettes, the macaroni tatters,
the dumplings in jam mayonnaise, a catapulting ordure of gross
and ramshackle shenanigans, openended paraphernalia. Follow me?
It all adds up. It's before you and behind you. I'm the only saviour
of the grace you find yourself wanting in. Mind how you go.
Look sharp. Get my drift? Don't let it get too mouldy. Watch the
mould. Get the feel of it, sonny, get the density. Look at me.

And I did.

VOICE 2. I am ill.

VOICE 1. It was like looking into a pit of molten lava, mother. One look
was enough for me.

VOICE 2. Come to me.

VOICE 1. I joined Mrs Withers for a Campari and soda in the kitchen.
She spoke of her youth. I was a right titbit, she said. I was like a
piece of plum duff. They used to come from miles to try their luck.
I fell head over heels with a man in the Fleet Air Arm. He adored me.
They had him murdered because they didn't want us to know
happiness. I could have married him and had tons of sons. But oh no.
He went down with his ship. I heard it on the wireless.

VOICE 2. I wait for you.

VOICE 1. Later that night Riley and I shared a cup of cocoa in his
quarters. I like slender lads, Riley said. Slender but strong. I've never
made any secret of it. But I've had to restrain myself, I've had to keep
a tight rein on my inclinations. That's because my deepest disposition
is towards religion. I've always been a deeply religious man. You can
imagine the tension this creates in my soul. I walk about in a constant
state of spiritual, emotional, psychological and physical tension. It's
breathtaking, the discipline I'm called upon to exert. My lust is
unimaginably violent but it goes against my best interests, which
are to keep on the right side of God. I'm a big man, as you see, I
could crush a slip of a lad such as you to death, I mean the death
that is love, the death I understand love to be. But meet it is that I
keep those desires shackled in handcuffs and leg-irons. I'm good at
that sort of thing because I'm a policeman by trade. And I'm highly

respected. I'm highly respected both in the force and in church. The only place where I'm not highly respected is in this house. They don't give a shit for me here. Although I've always been a close relation. Of a sort. I'm a fine tenor but they never invite me to sing. I might as well be living in the middle of the Sahara desert. There are too many women here, that's the trouble. And it's no use talking to Baldy. He's well away. He lives in another area, best known to himself. I like health and strength and intelligent conversation. That's why I took a fancy to you, chum, apart from the fact that I fancy you. I've got no-one to talk to. These women treat me like a leper. Even though I am a relation. Of a sort.

What relation?

Is Lady Withers Jane's mother or sister?

If either is the case why isn't Jane called Lady Jane Withers? Or perhaps she is. Or perhaps neither is the case? Or perhaps Mrs Withers is actually the Honorable Mrs Withers? But if that is the case what does that make Mr Withers? And which Withers is he anyway? I mean what relation is he to the rest of the Witherses? And who is Riley?

But if you find me bewildered, anxious, confused, uncertain and afraid, you also find me content. My life possesses shape. The house has a very warm atmosphere, as you have no doubt gleaned. And as you have no doubt noted from my account I talk freely to all its inhabitants, with the exception of Mr Withers, to whom no-one talks, to whom no-one refers, with evidently good reason. But I rarely leave the house. No-one seems to leave the house. Riley leaves the house but rarely. He must be a secret policeman. Jane continues to do a great deal of homework while not apparently attending any school. Lady Withers never leaves the house. She has guests. She receives guests. Those are the steps I hear on the stairs at night.

VOICE 3. I know your mother has written to you to tell you that I am dead. I am not dead. I am very far from being dead, although lots of people have wished me dead, from time immemorial, you especially. It is you who have prayed for my death, from time immemorial. I have heard your prayers. They ring in my ears. Prayers yearning for my death. But I am not dead.

Well, that is not entirely true, not entirely the case. I'm lying. I'm leading you up the garden path, I'm playing about, I'm having my bit of fun, that's what. Because I am dead. As dead as a doornail. I'm writing to you from my grave. A quick word for old time's sake. Just to keep in touch. An old hullo out of the dark. A last kiss from Dad.

I'll probably call it a day after this canter. Not much more to say. All a bit of a sweat. Why am I taking the trouble? Because of you,

I suppose, because you were such a loving son. I'm smiling, as I lie in this glassy grave.

Do you know why I use the word glassy? Because I can see out of it.

Lots of love, son. Keep up the good work.

There's only one thing bothers me, to be quite frank. While there is, generally, absolute silence everywhere, absolute silence throughout all the hours, I still hear, occasionally, a dog barking. I hear this dog. Oh, it frightens me.

VOICE 1. They have decided on a name for me. They call me Bobo. Good morning, Bobo, they say, or, See you in the morning, Bobo, or, Don't drop a goolie, Bobo, or, Don't forget the diver, Bobo, or, Keep your eye on the ball, Bobo, or, Keep this side of the tramlines, Bobo, or, How's the lead in your pencil, Bobo, or, How's tricks in the sticks, Bobo, or, Don't get too much gum in your gumboots, Bobo.

The only person who does not call me Bobo is the old man. He calls me nothing. I call him nothing. I don't see him. He keeps to his room. I don't go near it. He is old and will die soon.

VOICE 2. The police are looking for you. You may remember that you are still under twenty-one. They have issued your precise description to all the organs. They will not rest, they assure me, until you are found. I have stated my belief that you are in the hands of underworld figures who are using you as a male prostitute. I have declared in my affidavit that you have never possessed any strength of character whatsoever and that you are palpably susceptible to even the most blatant form of flattery and blandishment. Women were your downfall, even as a nipper. I haven't forgotten Françoise the French maid or the woman who masqueraded under the title of governess, the infamous Miss Carmichael. You will be found, my boy, and no mercy will be shown to you.

VOICE 1. I'm coming back to you, mother, to hold you in my arms.

I am coming home.

I am coming also to clasp my father's shoulder. Where is the old boy? I'm longing to have a word with him. Where is he? I've looked in all the usual places, including the old summer-house, but I can't find him. Don't tell me he's left home at his age? That would be inexpressibly skittish a gesture, on his part. What have you done with him, mother?

VOICE 2. I'll tell you what, my darling. I've given you up as a very bad job. Tell me one last thing. Do you think the word love means anything?

VOICE 1. I am on my way back to you. I am about to make the journey back to you. What will you say to me?

VOICE 3. I have so much to say to you. But I am quite dead. What I have to say to you will never be said.

BEEF

by David Pownall

For Michael McKay

David Pownall was born in Liverpool in 1938. He was educated at Lord Wandsworth College and the University of Keele. After graduating, he worked in personnel management at Ford Motor Company, then emigrated to Northern Rhodesia a year before Independence where he stayed for six years, employed in the copper mining industry. In 1969 he returned to England and, after two years with Century Theatre on tour in the north-west, he became a full-time novelist and playwright. In 1975 he founded the new-play touring company, Paines Plough with John Adams. Between 1972-76 he was resident playwright at the Duke's Playhouse, Lancaster. His novels are *The Raining Tree War, African Horse, God Perkins, Light On A Honeycomb* and, most recently, *Beloved Latitudes,* published in 1981 by Gollancz. His theatre plays include *Music to Murder By, Motocar, Richard the Third Part Two* (National Theatre, Cottesloe), *An Audience Called Edouard* (Greenwich) and *Livingstone and Sechele* (Traverse, Edinburgh; Lyric Studio, Hammersmith). He has written seventeen radio plays for the BBC, the most recent being *The Mist People,* produced by Alfred Bradley.

Beef was first broadcast on BBC Radio 3 on 9th April 1981. The cast was as follows:

CUSACK	Richard Leech
MAEVE	Fiona Victory
CON	Garrett Keogh
CUCKOO	Gerard Mannix Flynn
ALI	Sean Caffrey
FERGUS	James Donnelly
JANET	Anne Haydn

Director: Ian Cotterell

An abattoir yard. Fade in the buzzing of an electric razor. The buzzing stops. There is a click and the sound of the cuttings being blown out of the razor. Fade out.

CUSACK. Good people, good morning! If I used a cut-throat razor on meself this morning it would live up to its name. It was a wild old time in Dublin last night. Missed the last bus home and slept here at the abattoir, my place of work, having my own key as a trusted man. A question for you: would someone who made his bed in a slaughterhouse be haunted by the ghosts of cattle?

Fade back the abattoir atmosphere. A key turns in the lock of the personnel door in the big yard gate.

Ah, that'll be Mr Sheehan. No flies on him, I can tell you.

The door opens, then closes with a bang. But the lock is not set.

Good morning, Mr Sheehan.

CON. Morning Cusack! What do you make the time?

CUSACK. A quarter past seven.

CON. What's happening then? Where's the rest of the lads?

CUSACK. Give yourself time to arrive, Mr Sheehan . . .

CON. Everyone should be getting ready by now. We have a busy day ahead of us.

CUSACK. Don't start getting het up now. Relax for a minute.
Mr Sheehan, you know that we've been doing these Sunday overtime shifts on worn-out cattle all this year and, nothing daunted, you called another for today of all days.

CON. The whole of Irish industry can't grind to a halt just because the Pope's here, you know.

CUSACK. Oh, agreed! But on Friday there were mutterings from the locker room when I put it to the lads that they might turn out this morning.

CON. I did anticipate resistance from the genuinely devout churchgoers; i.e., none of them. They wouldn't turn down eight hours at double-time twelve weeks from Christmas, not these greedy beggars.

CUSACK. Mr Sheehan, as I was circulating in the city last night, traipsing round from house of religion to house of religion in search of peace, I bumped into the lads, many of them on their knees, and I got the impression that none of them had the slightest intention of reporting here for work this morning.

CON. Are you saying that we haven't got a shift?

CUSACK. The great mass that the Pope held in the Phoenix Park was just too much for them, and the little masses that followed well into the night obliterated all sense of practical reality.

CON. Is everyone who's employed here an alcoholic or something?

CUSACK. Oh, be fair, Mr Sheehan. You've been working them hard lately. They haven't had a day off for months.

CON. They get paid don't they? What more do they want?

CUSACK. You must be making a packet out of this work we do on the side. Couldn't you give the staff a backhander once in a while?

CON. That's neither here nor there, is it? Are we working today or not?

CUSACK. All, right. I just thought I'd mention it. Don't worry. I fixed everything.

CON. With no labour? Who's going to do the job? You and me? Listen, those two bulls we've got coming in are colossal creatures, old as the hills, tough as nails. It will take every man we've got to handle them.

CUSACK. Mr Sheehan, everything is under control. Last night I moved around in the twilight world I favour for a Saturday night out. I like a wander into the old haunts that haven't changed for centuries. The talk is good and the music unparalleled. You can get any job you like done down there. All you have to do is put the word out on the grapevine.

CON. Don't tell me you mean casuals?

CUSACK. Fine men, in general. Devils for work.

CON. Christ almighty, Cusack! You can't use casuals in highly-specialised slaughtering! I need trained men!

CUSACK. And you'll have them. I put the word out that only experts need bother to turn up.

CON. What about the union? They'll go mad.

CUSACK. I squared it with the union. They're not bothered. They say that if our lads don't want the overtime and it's an urgent job, then we should use temporary labour.

CON. I'm very doubtful, Cusack, old son. It strikes me that you've made a mess of the arrangements.

CUSACK. I haven't. Everything will be all right.

CON. You know this contract is for our biggest customer.

CUSACK. The importance of the job has not escaped me. I wouldn't disappoint a British pet-food company for the world.

CON. If we let them down . . .

CUSACK. Unthinkable. Unthinkable. Would I heap more pain and frustration on the heads of people with licensing laws like they've got?

The sound of a newspaper being unfolded and shaken out. Pause.

CUSACK. Your Sunday newspaper is a thick and juicy one, plenty of colour in it today.

CON. I like to keep up-to-date, as you know. No doubt your own choice of literature is more mind improving.

CUSACK. Literature? D'you think I'd call this literature? Never!

The pages of a book being riffled.

CUSACK. Solid sex and violence. Not recommended for children or those of delicate sensibilities. To be kept away from those who cannot stand the sight of blood, like yourself.

CON. Lay off, will you Cusack?

The newspaper being shaken with irritation.

CUSACK. Who else would the authorities make boss of a slaughterhouse over my head.

The book being riffled.

CUSACK. You should try reading this book, perhaps, Mr Sheehan. It might improve your knowledge of the world today, even though it was written way back. It's an old Irish fantasy called *The Cattle Raid of Cooley*. It will make you laugh, so it will. It's all lies and exaggerations, lies for the enjoyment of idiots.

CON. Idiots like you?

CUSACK. Idiots like me? No, idiots like all of us, Mr Sheehan, all of us.

CON. I'll stick to my paper, if you don't mind. (*Pause.*) Well, it looks as though the Pope has become a national hero overnight. The man is a veritable star. I see he's off in the old helicopter to the monastery at Clonmacnois this morning.

CUSACK. Did you get to the mass in the Phoenic Park yesterday?

CON. No, I watched it at home on the box. Very moving. I admire this Pope tremendously. You could feel the integrity and radiance coming out of him, and that being said by a man with no religion. I tell you, he has the power and charisma to change the political situation in Ireland right now. There's a great mood of optimism running through the country.

CUSACK. You're right. It was there last night until closing-time.

CON. The gunmen will be listening and watching everything that he does and says on television. It will affect them, you'll see.

CUSACK. The gunmen? Whoever thought they watched TV? Their behaviour would be ten times worse if they did. I think they'd be a lot better off with a good read of the old *Cattle Raid of Cooley*.

The book is riffled. The uproar of drunks at a distance.

CON. Will you listen to that? People going off to early morning mass in that condition. Is it any wonder that some of us turn to science for comfort?

CUSACK. Atrocious behaviour. Quite unforgivable.

CON. Do you know, they calculate that by the time the Pope leaves he will have been seen, in the flesh, by three quarters of the people of Ireland?

CUSACK. And here you have the consequences roaming the streets.

The uproar of drunks getting nearer.

CON. Straight out of the boozer into the church.

A rattle of bones.

CUCKOO. Death, blood and fury.

CON. Aaah! Get away! (*Pause.*) Where the hell did you spring from?

CUCKOO. I did the jump over the poisoned stroke and made it a little higher than usual. I think I'll have to open that door.

CON. As soon as you like, my friend, then get out of here.

CUCKOO. White bones, staring sockets, flowers in skulls. What a morning.

CON. On your way then, and good luck to you.

The sound of the door in the gate being opened.

CUCKOO. Come in, come in.

ALI. Is this the place, Cuckoo?

Chinking, rattling. Pause.

CON. Good God!

CUCKOO. This is the place.

FERGUS. Good. I've carried this for enough.

The sound of a big bundle being dropped with a crash. It rattles.

CON. Hey, don't put your stuff down now. You're not stopping. About turn you lot and out!

Chinking, rattling. A little mild laughter.

CON. Look, I'm instructing you to get off this property! You're trespassing! (*Pause.*) Well, don't just stand there with your mouth open, Cusack, do something!

CUSACK. What, exactly?

CON. Get these piss-heads out of here.

CUSACK. All right, all right. It's only a bunch of lads having a laugh. What would you say you were, eh? Mods, rockers, skin-heads, or just travelling people? Don't get excited now, Mr Sheehan. Leave them to me. Now, what would a collection of obvious vegetarians like yourselves be doing in a place of this nature?

ALI. There's an important job that needs to be done. We're here to do it.

CUSACK. What kind of a job?

ALI. Slaughtering.

CUSACK. Mr Sheehan, I think we have been found by the casuals.

CON. No, I'm not having that drunken rabble in here. Go on, hop it!

CUSACK. Do you know the work?

ALI. As good as anyone ever did.

CUSACK. Cash in hand. No question asked. I think these are good lads, Mr Sheehan. I like the look of the four of them.

CON. No, definitely! They're filthy dirty.

CUSACK. A good scrub and some disinfectant will cure that. Once we've got them in the white coats and the white wellies with the rubber gloves on they'll be unrecognisable from ordinary clean and decent people.

CON. They stink. These clothes are falling off them.

CUSACK. Oh, we can't afford to be choosy today, Mr Sheehan. Now, will you supervise them directly, yourself, or shall I appoint a leader from within the group?

MAEVE. I'm already their leader, and don't you forget it.

CON. It's a woman under all that clobber! A bloody woman!

ALI. Maeve will supervise.

MAEVE. Naturally, Ali, naturally.

CON. I'm not having a woman working here!

MAEVE. What have you got against women? Not your weapon I'll be bound.

CON. That's it! Enough is enough.

CUSACK. Leave it to me, Mr Sheehan. I'm sorting it out for you, aren't I?

CON. I don't know what's got into you today, Cusack.

CUCKOO (*chanting*).
Heads hacked off, blood spurting,
Swords crashing, men screaming,
Heroes dealing death like cards!

CON. All right, all right. My clerk here will settle this. It's in your hands, Cusack.

Slight fade.

CUSACK. Well, you're a sight for sore eyes, my friends. I'm glad you could make it.

MAEVE. We made the beginning, Cusack. It is only right that we should make the end.

CUCKOO. I heard the Pope give the druid's snapping-mouth and the high hero's scream down in Drogheda yesterday.

ALI. It was a great moment, Cuckoo, wasn't it, my boy? Yes, he demanded a change in us all. Speaking in a voice of thunder which could be heard for miles, he shouted that the old times were over. Then he flew into the air, roaring and swaying in the wind.

FERGUS. You know how long we've waited for peace, Cusack. No one will believe it but the hero longs for nothing else, so he can rest and dream of the old days. He does not want his deeds repeated. Isn't that so, Ali?

CON. I'm leaving it to you, Cusack, old son, just as you said . . .

MAEVE. The bulls are on the move then?

CUSACK. At first light this morning they started out.

MAEVE. I can feel the land tensed up, waiting for the brunt of it.

CUSACK. It will be a blow of catastrophic proportions.

CUCKOO (*chanting*).
 The great brown bull of Ulster,
 The huge white bull of the South;
 Ravens have followed them always,
 Women have grieved while filling
 Their hoof-marks with tears
 Where they roam are the roads of blood.

CON. Cusack, old son . . . make a move, eh? Out, if you don't mind.
 Now. Immediately . . .

FERGUS (*chanting*).
 The field of slaughter bloomed red
 with body-flowers, white with bone-blossoms
 blue with staring eyes, green with bile,
 brown with bowel; all the colours
 were there to entertain the ravens,
 kindle the kite's appetite.

CUCKOO. There will be such a shuddering! Such a shaking! Great
 feats of strength! (*To* CON:) Would you like to see me do the
 hardest feat of all? Stepping on a spear in flight, then straightening
 erect on its point.

CON. Lad, I'm sorry for you. You're wasting your breath.

CUCKOO. Climbing up a spear then performing a dance on its point
 without making the soles of the feet bleed? It's easy when you know
 how.

CON. Is it indeed? No doubt you're the only man in the world who
 can strike a match on wet soap. Push off, will you?

CUCKOO. We're not wanted, Maeve. All that journey for nothing.
 They don't want us. What do they care about the bulls?

MAEVE. We'll do what we came to do. Help him. Don't let him
 get into his doom-slide. Come now, Cuckoo. What do we care if
 we're wanted or not? Did we expect a great reception when it has
 all been spent on the Pope? We just have our task to perform.

CUCKOO. Who will watch us? Who cares?

MAEVE. History will care, and the future.

ALI. Come, rest your head, Cuckoo. Remember how hard it is to be
 a hero in your own time, never mind someone else's.

MAEVE. His hair is as rough as a winter thorn bush. Well, we brought
 something of our own with us. They last well, these lice. Your
 hair is teeming with them Cuckoo . . .

CON. Oh no, lice! In here! We'll have to go through the whole
 place with a fumigator . . . Do something, Cusack! They're crawling
 with vermin!

MAEVE. The big ones are helping the little ones over the gaps between the hairs. Why, here's a crowd camped just above the curve of your ear. They're lighting fires, cooking meat, posting sentries . . .

ALI. Oooooh, Cuckoo, I can see a hundred heroes in here arming themselves before dawn, strapping on harness, rubbing grease into their chariot-axles. Whay! Here's a gang of stone-slingers, whirling away in your head. Get ready to duck!

CON. Cusack!

CUSACK. Sssssssssh! You're taking a risk with yourself, Mr Sheehan.

CON. Bloody vermin! They'll be leaping all over the premises. Look, Cusack, old son, these ruffians are a health-hazard. Get rid of them!

A low, constant musical humming.

CUCKOO. We should go back, Maeve. It won't work.

MAEVE. It will, I promise you. We will do it, together. Don't despair, Cuckoo. Your strength will still be needed. True courage is in short supply.

CON. Don't let the bastards fall asleep! We'll never get rid of them. They're not relatives of yours are they? Those nephews from Galway?

CUSACK. Oh, we all have a spot of their blood in our veins, Mr Sheehan. Aren't we all heroes on the sly, when no one is looking? But treat them carefully. They're not in a mood to be fooled with.

CON. Neither am I. As manager of this place . . .

CUSACK. Come off it, will you? All that's out in the open now. You stand exposed. Don't forget, I know . . . I know. There are more lice in your mind than there are in his head. D'you know what the staff call you?

CON. I don't. Nor do I care.

CUSACK. Can't you face a little truth like that?

Pause.

CON. Cusack, old son, er . . . I can see that I've upset you somehow. I must admit, I don't know why . . .

CUSACK. They call you 'Slackarse'.

CON. Good of them. Cusack, old son, is it anything to do with that salary increase I put you up for but you didn't get. Now that wasn't my fault . . .

CUSACK. Don't worry. I remember your heroic battle on my behalf. Mr Sheehan, your in-tray is a gaping void and your out-tray is a yawning chasm. In between is the Desert of Eternity.

CUCKOO. Cusack, Cusack . . . I don't like this place. I don't like the smell. Couldn't we ambush the bulls on the road? Look at it . . . none of the colour and encrustation of the old spots of sacrifice. It doesn't feel right. For death, it's too clean, too clean.

CUSACK (*to* CON). I will make a confession to you. If you were a man of any religion I might stand a chance of being believed in the sin which I must reveal. But you, with your analytical mind, will merely become incredulous, not being trained to the lewd and impossible as is the ear of a priest. Amongst my sins there is one that is paramount. It towers above all the others. It is an unnatural sin. It is a sin that creates more sin, in envy. There is no worse sin in the world, and I have suffered for it. Without blessing, without permission, by a twist of Time and Nature, I have lived over eight hundred years. Disgusting, isn't it?

CON. Eight hundred years? Quite a night you must have had, Cusack, old son. You might have said you were still motherless . . .

CUSACK. Don't look my age, do I? Want to know my secret?

CON. Behave like a prick if you want to, but I've had enough! Now, this is your last chance, Cusack. I'm giving you a direct order. Help me get these people out of here.

CUSACK. No.

CON. Right. I'm putting you on a formal charge of refusing to obey a lawful instruction.

CUSACK. I couldn't care less, but here's the right form for you to fill in. Three copies, remember. And don't forget to press hard with your biro or it doesn't come through.

FERGUS. Maeve . . . will we ever get back?

MAEVE. No, Fergus, my love. Once we've done the job and the air has been cleared, I think we will fade away.

FERGUS. Where to, Maeve?

MAEVE. Some bone-yard somewhere. Peaceful enough. The idea is for us to be forgotten about. Cusack has told you, Fergus, heroes like us are redundant. We have to get out of the way. Death is best for us four.

ALI. But the great druid, the flying John Paul who stands on a spear and straightens erect on its point, surely that man is a hero? Look at his hands. Look at his head. Look how he circles the world checking his honour like a farmer checks his fence-posts.

MAEVE. Ah, he is a true hero of today, Cusack says. On his back he does not carry harness but ideas. In his hands he has no weapons, only the record of his talk. In his eyes are mirrors to reflect the questions. He does not prophesy, nor visit oracles. He shouts only the known words.

FERGUS. Could we try again, Maeve? (*Pause*.) Oh, I've made you sad.

CUSACK. You must forgive them if they slip and slide in your scientific brain, Mr Sheehan. Like new-born infants, they're covered in mild, metaphorical jelly, incapable of standing still and making Anglo-Saxon sense. Pity them. The ground was never steady under their feet. All impulse you see. No plan, except for today, and I sketched that one out for them.

CON. So you are responsible?

CUSACK. Oh, you know how responsible I am, Mr Sheehan.

CON. You and me will have things to talk about once this is over. I think all I can do now is phone for the police.

CUSACK. Fair enough.

CON. Well, perhaps I'll give it a bit longer to sort it out. But I'm not laughing, Cusack, old son, not laughing at all.

CUSACK. I should hope not. Me and my friends are very serious about what we're doing.

CON. Which is what, exactly?

CUSACK. In all your reading up there in the office while the killing was going on under your feet but out of your mind, did you ever get round to any yarns about the Irish heroes of old, such as I've got in my book.

CON. I can't say I did.

CUSACK. Well, you might be equally indifferent to meeting them now — Queen Maeve and King Ali of Connaught, Fergus her lover, betrayer of Ulster, and Cuckoo — the hero of Ulster. Now, I'm eight hundred years old and I don't feel a day over forty, but they're knocking on two thousand — hence the smell.

CON. The smell I believe in.

CUSACK. They were the authors of their own deeds. What actions they took rattled in the air until it got hot and radiant. The reverberations never died away in Ireland, not from the first century until the Normans came. People kept them alive by word of mouth only. Now me, I was unemployed at the end of the twelfth century — always a traditionalist, you see — and my parents put me in the monastery at Clonmacnois on the east bank of the Shannon. Hired as a man of prayer, I found myself frustrated as I had no faith in Anglo-Norman Christianity and couldn't open my mouth to an alien god. One day the Bishop of Leinster found me idling around and said, 'Give that lazy sod something to do.' 'What?', says the brother in charge of me. The Bishop thought for a minute and then said — conscious as he was of the great cultural changes taking place and the danger of the people losing their identity — 'Let him collect and write down the full text of the *'The Cattle Raid of Cooley*' from the lips of the peasants.'

CUCKOO. I had a house made from human heads. All my windows were made from the hip-bones of queens and my lintels from the thigh-bones of priests. That was what people said of me, and that was what was true.

CON. Who would waste time doubting it? (*Pause.*) Cusack . . . I don't think you're yourself today. I know you have a habit of picking up strange companions in your wanderings on a Saturday night, but bringing them to work is well past my sense of humour.

CUSACK. You interpret my old routines correctly. I am a lonely man. I do love a drink and a talk, and I do get enthusiastic about new friends. All this I admit. Ask my landlady. (*Pause.*) But these are the heroes.

MAEVE. What time are the bulls due?

CUSACK. Eight o'clock.

MAEVE. And you're sure they're the ones?

CUSACK. The White Bull of the South and the Brown Bull of Ulster.

MAEVE. Did you tell the drivers that if they get the bulls here on time there'd be largesse in it for them — the use of my friendly thighs?

CUSACK. Maeve, what would stop them speeding and taking chances with their cargo if I told them that? They're simple men.

MAEVE. I want the scheme to work, Cusack. We didn't come here for nothing.

CUSACK. I've done everything I could. Do you think the Pope will understand a tribute like this? He's not one for sacrificing beasts on altars.

MAEVE. Ach, come off it. Everybody is.

CUSACK. The carcases are intended for the British dogmeat trade. You don't mind that?

MAEVE. Let the flesh look after itself. It's the thought behind the sword that counts. The lives of those two old bulls will go out like a pair of summer storms. They'll do the job, put the pressure in the right place.

CUSACK. But how will I persuade this dimwit that we're telling the truth?

CON. Christ, Cusack, old son — you hate me, don't you? All these years I've spent sticking up for you and this is the thanks I get . . .

CUCKOO. Fight him. Weapons. Blood. Hacking. Heads flying. Revenge. Watch the crows peck out his eyes. Put his head over your door to smile for ever. Hate will get you high up. High up. Yaaah!

The door in the gate opens and then bangs shut.

JANET. Oh, I was looking for Mr Sheehan . . .

CUCKOO. This is the country where I would rest my weapon.

JANET. Are you talking to me?

CUCKOO. Would you lend me the loan of your apples?

CON. Er . . . over here, Miss Soames. Sorry about this . . .

JANET. I apologise for the intrusion, Mr Sheehan. I was passing so I thought I'd check that everything was all right with our order. Everything is all right, is it? No problems have arisen, I hope.

CON. Well, the beasts haven't arrived yet.

JANET. Haven't they?

MAEVE. We're all waiting for them, impatiently. This man will tell you. He's lucky to have us.

CON. These people are nothing to do with me, Miss Soames. They're just trouble-makers. You know, last night the whole of Dublin was on its ear. They just came in off the street. I'm sorry.

JANET. Well, I hope you manage to get rid of them soon. My company is looking forward to the order being met in a satisfactory manner. Being importuned by vagrants will not be accepted as a reasonable excuse.

MAEVE. Vagrants? Do you think we haven't got a home to go to?

JANET. I hope everything works out, Mr Sheehan. I'll ring you in the morning when your premises have been washed out. Ten o'clock at number three dock.

MAEVE. Why is this woman leaving us so soon? She interests me.

JANET. I'd like to go now, if you don't mind.

FERGUS. Maeve wants to get to know you better.

MAEVE. Bring her over here.

JANET. Put me down, you brute!

MAEVE. Look at the hips on her. Now, would a child get through here, never mind an army?

JANET. Get off me! Mr Sheehan!

CON. Hey, cut that out! You, woman, leave her alone!

Three swords being drawn.

FERGUS. Don't you address the queen as *woman*. Unsay that!

CON. Look, there's no need for . . .

FERGUS. Unsay it!

CON. Sorry, sorry. Now, will you put your blades away? Now, somebody must tell us what's going on.

JANET. It's obvious, isn't it? I know what I'm dealing with. Well, should we get down to business!

CUSACK. Business, Miss Soames?

JANET. Of course.

CUSACK. What business?

JANET. Look, I've been expecting something like this to happen for a long time. My company has always known that having an office in Ireland is risky. We've been prepared. The personnel department has issued a pamphlet with clear instructions to all staff as to what steps we should take and how we should behave.

CUSACK. Miss Soames, you're misjudging these characters here. All they've come for is to do a slaughtering job.

JANET. You have taken us hostage. What else could it be? (*Pause.*) It has all the signs. (*Pause.*) You have taken us hostage, haven't you?

MAEVE. I think the woman wants us to say yes.

CUSACK. A pamphlet is a powerful thing.

JANET. The first step is for me to ascertain what you want from us. In writing, if possible . . .

MAEVE. Well, Cusack does all the writing for us . . .

CUSACK. Miss Soames, you're a natural born extremist, you know that?

JANET. You are holding us here, aren't you?

CUSACK. Long enough to pass the time of day, that's all . . .

JANET. That's what they all say. You wouldn't tell us that you intend to keep us here for ever. Now, come on, let's get down to it. What are your demands?

CON. All I can get out of them so far is that they want to work on the carcases for your consignment.

JANET. The bulls for this morning?

CON. That's right. They want nothing else out of life. See what I mean?

JANET. They're keeping us here so they can kill bulls? Everyone will think they're mad.

CON. Useful in court later on. It's a cover so they can plead insanity.

JANET. I insist on knowing! Are you from the IRA? The UDA? The UDF? The UFF? The UUU?

MAEVE. Is that a spell she's chanting? Are you chanting a spell at me? Don't act the druid if you haven't got the powers.

JANET. Why be so secretive about it? It's not fair! We must know.

CON. Cusack, for Christ's sake, find out what they want. We're not going to resist. If they're going to hold us hostage that's fine . . . these things can be arranged . . .

JANET. He's with them. There's no point in asking him for help.

CON. Cusack? Never. (*Pause.*) In spite of appearances I think the man is still loyal to me. He's been indoctrinated. It's tragic.

CUSACK. Don't get us wrong now. Mr Sheehan, I've reached the natural end of my employment here. There must be some other sucker in Dublin who could come along and run this place while you play the gentleman slaughterer, pretending the job isn't there. Failed his degree in Physics at Trinity, didn't you? You never got over the shock, did you Mr Sheehan? It induced a strange paralysis of the nine-to-five nervous system. Butchery is below him. And blood? That's something you use to encourage the growth of tomatoes.

JANET. We intend to co-operate in every way possible. Please, let us all keep calm. I have had instructions from my company head office that I am to avoid heroics . . .

CUCKOO. Yaaaah! Scream! Sword-edge and sloped shield! Thunder-feat!

JANET. Stop him yelling at me!

CUCKOO. I'll show you the spurt of speed, the stroke of precision! With my massive stroke-dealing sword I'll hack bits as big as babies' heads off those bulls. I'll strangle them with their own dewlaps!

CUSACK. All right, Cuckoo. They'll be here soon. Don't get impatient.

CUCKOO. Lumps like boulders I'll hack off!

JANET. He's a psychopath! Do something about him!

CUSACK. He's not interested in you. Did I tell you that I was eight hundred years old?

JANET. Will you please stop beating about the bush and tell us why these friends of yours want to kill our bulls so much?

MAEVE. Your bulls? What are you talking about?

CUSACK. Maeve, these two did arrange to buy the two bulls, not knowing what they were. You know what Irish farmers are like about the age of their stock.

JANET. But why do you have to come here for them?

ALI. Because this is the only place that people can sacrifice a beast these days. Anywhere else and there'd be trouble. It's quite a complicated business and it has to be done properly if it is going to work. The place has to be thoroughly prepared, the altar decorated in the correct manner, the right prayers have to be said, songs sung, music made. And, of course, the beasts must be killed with the necessary ritual otherwise the whole thing will fail.

JANET. Thank you for explaining all that to me. And what is the sacrifice for?

ALI. To help the Pope bring peace to Ireland, which is what everyone seems to want.

JANET. Well, I don't know what to say. What do you think, Mr Sheehan?

CON. Do you mean, will it work? I don't see why not. A bit of sacrifice doesn't do any harm, so we're told.

CUSACK. It improves the stock of political causes like roses thrive on horse manure.

MAEVE. You two have never seen a blood-stained altar, have you? Never seen the red fog rolling out of the bull's entrails into the clear air. We were brought up on it as children.

ALI. You can do a lot with death which you can't with life.

MAEVE. And our druids were thoughtful men, men who could take the initiative, like this Pope. Ours would try anything — anything — to get rid of a plague or a piece of bad luck which was affecting the people. They'd turn themselves inside-out, experiment, take chances with their own lives. I've seen druids who've fallen asleep at the altar, covered in blood, having sacrificed every sort of living creature they could until they found the right one. Sometimes it was as small as a mouse or a wren. They never gave up. (*Pause.*) We get the idea from all this show and shouting, that if this visit doesn't work, the Pope will think there is nothing else to be done. No one has told him about the bulls, you see. He doesn't know that they're still roaming around. (*Pause.*) He hasn't made them a part of his calculations.

CUSACK. Miss Soames, I still get the feeling that you're not with us body and soul. And even Mr Sheehan doesn't seem entirely convinced. So I will have to reveal all, down to the last detail. Today we are going to create what Ireland needs most. It's nothing very complicated. A child could understand it quite easily. You could work it out yourselves. (*Pause.*) What Ireland needs is a great natural disaster.

CUCKOO. Wham! Wham! Wham! Wham!

CUSACK. Irish disasters in the past have always been without flair or drama, having at their middles either vegetables or the seven virtues. But no natural cataclysms — nothing that just came out of the earth or the sky. Well, we're going to remedy that. I bet you can't guess what it is?

CON. Lagging far behind you, Cusack, old son, far behind you.

CUSACK. We're going to make an earthquake.

CON. An earthquake? Are you now?

CUSACK. Followed by a tidal wave of such huge proportions that it will wash out the country from coast to coast. (*Pause.*) Isn't it on the tip of your tongue to ask us how we're going to do that? (*Pause.*) I thought it was. When the Pope jams himself into the cramped little cell at Clonmacnois where I first wrote down the stories of these heroes and made immortal the violence of an older Ireland there will obviously be a major disturbance. But that would not be quite enough to split the earth. So we're going to sacrifice those two terrible, ridiculous, discredited old bulls and project their tormented souls into the same supernatural forcefield as the Pope at the precise moment of his entry into my old cell at Clonmacnois. With Ireland more sensitive to reverberations today than any other for two thousand years, it cannot help but produce a convulsion of the beloved, suffering earth which will shake the Irish down to the back teeth, together. That's the thing. Together. (*Pause.*) I haven't got through to you, Miss Soames?

JANET. Yes, yes. The Irish must be shaken. I'm all for it, honestly.

MAEVE. Oooh, come on, let's get started. This waiting is itching my insides.

ALI. Now, you two disbelievers, best to keep out of the way while we do this. And don't interrupt. That's a blasphemy for which you could be made to suffer.

Rattle of the bones. Low humming.

MAEVE. Clonmacnois!

Fade sound effects of the abattoir. Fade in an atmosphere of MAEVE's *mind.*

Can the earth hear my voice calling? It can.

Fade out the atmosphere of MAEVE's *mind. Fade in the abattoir atmosphere.*

Suffering Mother Earth, we have two great bulls to bring you peace. Accept them as the great druid and Pope stands on you at the place where we were written down to live for ever.

Fade the abattoir atmosphere. Fade in the atmosphere of MAEVE's *mind.*

Yes. The earth is listening. I know it.

Fade out the atmosphere of MAEVE's *mind. Fade in the abattoir atmosphere.*

Rattle of the bones.

CUCKOO (*chanting*). First will be the Brown Bull of Ulster! Dark, dire, devilish, handsome with health, horrible, hairy, furiously fierce, full of cunning, glowing with guile. Thirty grown men can stand on his back in a line! A beast enormous! A beast for breeding blood.

Rattle of the bones.

MAEVE (*chanting*). Then will come the White Bull of the South. Finnbennach, with his useless tits struck flat against his colossal belly of brawn. As he gambols, his weapon scythes the sweet grass, sharpened for slitting heifers and cows. Bellowing his pleasure he smells the future union.

Rattle of the bones.

ALI (*chanting*). I ask the air to take the souls of these two creatures, to ferry them through cloud and rain, over rivers, and hills crossing the green land to place them at the feet of Mother Earth at Clonmacnois!

Rattle of the bones.

FERGUS (*chanting*). Blood is sweet to the earth, the living wine of life. We are the sons and daughters of the mother of all men. Mother, these will be the greatest beasts of Ireland, slain for you. All we ask is that you tremble as you drink.

The humming fades.

CUCKOO. It's the smell I can't stand, the smell of trees, pine trees, but no forest. Where's the forest? Who's taken the trees?

CON. Look, I'll give them a full day's pay, double-time, to leave us alone. I want to close up now. Sorry, Miss Soames, the shipment won't be made tomorrow.

CUSACK. You will have to stay until the bulls are slaughtered.

CON. Cusack, old son . . .

JANET. We undertake to leave here and not go to the police. Agreed, Mr Sheehan?

CON. Absolutely. You can trust us.

CUCKOO.
I can smell the forest but there are no trees!
I can smell the forest but there are no leaves!
I can smell the forest but there are no roots!

CUCKOO *starts to snarl, yelp, growl and sigh. Then his breath goes into long, shuddering gasps and groans.*

CON. Control the bastard, can't you? He's going off his rocker!

CUCKOO *whimpers like a puppy, sniffs, growls.*

JANET. He's getting ready to do it again. He's making himself do it, the animal! Oh God . . .

CUCKOO *bays, growls, snarls, spits in a furious convulsion. When his fury has spent itself he is left breathing deeply, whimpering, crying. Pause.*

MAEVE. The power is still in him. That was a good warp-spasm, Cuckoo. The Hound of Ulster still lives in you.

CUSACK. What did you think of that, Miss Soames?

JANET. I presume it was some kind of fit.

CON. Ach, it's drying-out time. Sunday morning and the eight o'clock horrors.

CUSACK. You hear them, Maeve? Cuckoo put on his warp-spasm and it's a fit. Did I not tell you the truth when I said terror was dead?

MAEVE. In my own court I took the heads off people who deliberately blinded themselves. Self-mutilation is a sin. Now, you were here when Cuckoo was in the toils of his warp-spasm, weren't you?

CON. Yes, yes, of course.

ALI. Will you pardon me if I suggest that you might have overlooked the fact that he became a monstrous article, vile, terrible and shapeless?

CON. Yes, yes, I did notice . . .

FERGUS. And did you notice how his shanks and his joints, every knuckle and knee-bone, every angle and artery and organ from top to bottom shook like a tree in the flood or a reed in the stream? Woman! You saw all that?

JANET. Yes. Of course.

MAEVE. Good. No doubt you were enthralled and entertained with the way his whole body made a tearing twist inside his skin so that all his flesh was loosened and wallowed around in him like a new-born pig in a bag. And did you see his feet, knees and shins switch round until they were facing the wrong way? The balled sinews of his calves flew round like big knots on a ship's rope. On his mighty head the veins of his temples writhed . . . didn't they?

JANET. If you say so.

MAEVE. Oh, I do, I do. Just as I say that the sinews of his neck gathered into a knob the size of a month-old child's head and his face and features were thrust back until they became a deep, red bowl. You caught that?

JANET. Yes. Yes. If that's what you want, yes.

ALI. Did you see that special feature of his then? He sucked one eye so deep into his skull that a wild crane couldn't get at it with its long beak probing!

CON. Yes, we saw that too.

FERGUS. The other popped out of the socket and dangled there like a bell's clapper bumping against the cheek-bone. His mouth grew wider and wider in a terrible cave of distortion until all the skin was unrolled from the jaw and out heaved his liver and lungs from the gullet, flapping there like a great red flag while flakes of flaming blood flew all round his head. No doubt you captured these moments as well?

JANET. Yes, yes, yes.

MAEVE. This is truly a day of hope. Now I am sure that they must be capable of seeing the last and most terrible sign of the hero's warp-spasm.

MAEVE. Over Ireland, in the clear air, as high as a whale will throw the ocean, or a boy will throw a ball, from the very dead centre of his skull, will rise a fountain of blood.

A terrible cry from CUCKOO. *The roar of a great gush of blood which rises to a crescendo, then fades away. Fade out the abattoir atmosphere.*

CUSACK. Good people, never mind the hero's blood. There's plenty more where that came from. I'll give you something more worth your sympathy — me, in the old days at the monastery of Clonmacnois when I was still young — sixty at the most — collecting the stories of the heroes to put in my book of *The Cattle Raid of Cooley.*

Fade in the sound of a Gregorian chant at a distance. It is CUSACK's *cell at Clonmacnois. The door is open.*

CUSACK. Come in, come in all of you.

The sniffing, coughing and muttering of peasants. The door of the cell is slammed. The Gregorian chant is shut off. A very claustrophobic atmosphere. Every sound is audible — pen on sheepskin; breathing.

CUSACK. Right, snippets of the heroes. If you peasants have rested and cleaned up after your journeys here to Clonmacnois, let us start.

FERGUS. Will we have the money first?

CUSACK. You will not. Money comes after the information. Who's first?

FERGUS. That's me.

MAEVE. It is not! I got here long before you. Did you not see me sitting here getting my thoughts together?

CUSACK. Well then, young woman. What do you know of the story of the two Bulls of Ireland?

MAEVE. I know a small portion.

CUSACK. What about?

MAEVE. Queen Maeve.

CUSACK. Let's hope you've got something good to say about her. All I've got so far is the most unmitigated filth.

MAEVE. Mine is a very simple and straightforward story illustrating the queen's essential humanity.

CUSACK. Well, that sounds very encouraging. Let's have it then.

MAEVE. It is soon told. Queen Maeve's son-in-law, Ferdia, was told to go out and fight the unbeatable Ulster hero, Cuckoo. Ferdia got himself ready and drove over in his chariot to say farewell. He did not think much of his chances of survival. At Maeve's tent he found her squatting in the darkness over something and saying, quite affectionately, 'Are you still asleep?'

CUSACK. 'Are you still asleep?'

MAEVE. My grandmother, from whom I learnt the story, thought that Maeve was pissing in the king's ear.

CUSACK. Why should she be doing that?

MAEVE. My grandmother said that it was the only way to talk to some men.

CUSACK. And that is your contribution?

MAEVE. I've walked fifty miles to tell it to you.

CUSACK. Here's your money. If you've got any more like that then leave them at home. Who's next?

FERGUS. That's me.

CUSACK. What story have you brought me?

FERGUS. The story of an encounter; a fight, if you like.

A heavy imperious knock at the door of the cell. CUSACK *tuts. The door is opened. Gregorian chant is heard.*

CUSACK. Your Grace!

CON. The holy sister here and myself would like to sit in on your work for a while.

JANET. Yes, I'm very interested in ancient Ireland.

CON. Please settle down again. Don't let us interrupt. Pretend that we're not here. Carry on now.

*The door of cell is slammed shut.
The Gregorian chant fades.* CUSACK *sighs.*

CUSACK. Get on with your story then. (*In a whisper*:) I hope it's an improvement on the last one!

FERGUS. Much better, brother monk, much better. It is soon told.

CUSACK. Get on with it then.

FERGUS. An Ulsterman called Ilech came against the army of the south at a place called Ath Feidli. His chariot was highly decrepit and falling to bits and it was pulled by two old jaundiced horses, spavined and knock-kneed to the degree where they could only shamble. Ilech had his old chariot full of stones and clods of earth and he threw these at the people who came to stare at him, for the old warrior was fighting stark naked and his worn-out weapon and bollocks hung down through a hole in the chariot floor, banging on the ground.

CUSACK. Oh God!

FERGUS. The army of the south jeered at Ilech and told him to get out of the way or they would trample on him. Ilech pulled his old worn-out weapon up and whirled it round his head, then cast it at the army of the south, catching a hundred warriors in a noose from which he hanged them from a tree while battering their brains out with his bollocks.

CUSACK. Have you finished?

FERGUS. That's the only bit I can remember.

CUSACK. Here's your money, though you don't deserve it. Your Grace, I apologise . . .

CON. Think nothing of it . . .

CUSACK. Your mistress' . . . sorry, the holy sister's ears . . . I wouldn't want to pollute them further . . . Your Grace, couldn't I be taken off this job and put on something else . . . breaking rocks, or digging ditches . . . anything, anything.

CON. Remember, my son, this is a pre-Christian poem we're dealing with. We can't expect the same high standards of decency as we observe ourselves.

CUSACK. But they only remember the filth! Why?

CON. Oh, to tease us. You know the Irish. They're probably making it up as they go along. We will have the opportunity to take a second look at it later and make suitable revisions.

CUSACK (*to* JANET). Please forgive them sister. They are lowly people with no idea of what they're saying.

JANET. I think it is charming, charming.

CUSACK. That's enlightened of you, sister. I fear there may be worse to come.

JANET. Nothing can shock me, brother. Before I came over from England I was trained in the ways of the Irish.

CUSACK. I could do with some of that myself. What mysteries did they explain?

JANET. Their natural courtesy and hospitality. Their good humour. Their particular sensitivities.

CUSACK. Aha! Could you enumerate for the sake of this rabble? They might learn something about themselves.

JANET. The Irish, I was told, have a highly-developed sense of wonder about human affairs. They are full of admiration for the business of being alive but often regret the intensity of the experience. They are prone to boiling over and overstatement.

CUSACK. Let it never be said!

JANET. Tremendous respect for family ties and bonds. An almost supernatural addiction to the ceremonies of death . . .

CUSACK. This is a course I must get on. Your Grace. Send me to England for a refresher.

CON. Your great work must not be disturbed, my son. England would only confuse you. As an Irishman born and bred you might find much in the life of such a highly civilised people which struck you as worthless, overpractical and mercenary. Stick with it.

CUSACK. All right, Your Grace, but I don't think it's fair. The last twenty years of my life I've spent writing down this appalling stuff. I'd rather wear a hair shirt and go in for flagellation. Next!

ALI. That's me, brother.

CUSACK. You have a story?

ALI. I do.

CUSACK. Is it in any way to do with bodily functions?

ALI. Mine is about healing.

CUSACK. Ah. That sounds more like it. Gentleness, mercy, understanding . . .

ALI. It is soon told. An Ulsterman called Cethern arrived at Cuckoo's camp with his guts round his feet after a fight. 'Get me a doctor,' he said. There were no Ulster doctors so Cuckoo sent word to the enemy to send one of theirs, and he came. When he saw Cethern's guts round his feet he said, 'You won't survive this.' 'Neither will you,' Cethern cried and fisted the doctor until the healing-man's brains splashed over his feet. Then Cuckoo found fifty more doctors to come to Cethern and they were all killed in the same way . . .

CUSACK (*interrupting*). Fifty?

ALI. Fifty. I can see my great-grandfather saying it now, a cup at his knee. Fifty.

CUSACK. Cethern killed fifty doctors for saying he wouldn't survive. Go on, go on.

ALI. The fifty-first doctor only got a glancing blow and Cuckoo saved his life.

CUSACK. Decent of him.

ALI. So Cuckoo sent to Ulster for a doctor and one called Fintin came from the King's own court. He looked at Cethern's injuries and said: 'The blood is black here. You were speared at an angle, right through the heart. All your guts have been cut off from each other and lie in a heap like a ball of wool, rolling round your body. I can't promise to cure you . . . '

CUSACK. So he killed him as well, splashing his brains over his feet.

ALI. Not at all, at all. Just hold your horses, brother, then the doctor Fintin went on to say: 'I'll tell you no lie, but your case is plain to me. A whole army has left its mark in your tripes and one way or another your life is nearly over. Either your wounds will have to be treated for a year and you'll live, or I can do it in three days and three nights and give you enough strength for one last fight. Take your pick!' (*Pause.*) Which choice did the Ulster warrior take, do you think?

CUSACK. You're telling the story.

ALI. What does the bishop say? Or the English nun? What does anyone say who's here? Don't we know what the man's choice was? (*Pause.*) Give me the strength for one last fight.

CON. I think we'll be going now, Cusack, my son. That was all very interesting, wasn't it, sister?

JANET. Absolutely gripping. I can't wait for the book to come out.

CON. Keep up the good work. Pax vobiscum.

JANET. Good night, and joy be with you all.

> *The door opens. Gregorian chant is heard.*
> *The door slams. Laughter.*

CUSACK. Wisht now. Don't be disrespectful. Well, I think that will be enough for tonight.

ALI. What about the boy here. He's not said a word since he came in.

CUSACK. That's up to him. I'm not forcing him if he's shy. Some people are like that. (*Pause.*) Tell me, all of you, are the sore feet worth it. All this way for what?

MAEVE. We know we're forgetting things more and more. The old world is dying on us.

CUSACK. But people will stay the same. You know what I've got so far, after years of work, tramping over the bogs, sitting here with all kinds from children to grandfathers? A poem in praise of thieves and liars and murderers. Why did you bother to remember it? Why did your fathers bother to pass it on?

MAEVE. How do you spend a dark night? There's the rain, the wind, the cows. Not much else . . . Hey, boy, isn't that so? (*Pause.*) Come on, talk to us. Where are you from?

CUCKOO. The feat of the javelin and the rope, snapping mouth, hero's scream, spurt of speed, stroke of precision.

The rattling of the bones. Fade Clonmacnois cell atmosphere.

CUSACK. Good people, if you're ever short of a job, don't take up monking for a living. In your solitude you will come hard up against the question: What does the natural animal mind of man love most? And it has an answer that will shake your bones. There's wisdom in that answer though, painful as the truth may be. What man loves most he has plenty of. Blood. No man is poor beside this item of his adoration. There is no imbalance in the possession of it. I have as much as you and the other way about.

Fade in the Clonmacnois cell atmosphere.

CUCKOO (*screaming*). Aaaaaaah! Wha . . .

CUSACK. What is it, lad?

CUCKOO. Wham! Wham! Wham! Wham! My heart is going.

CUSACK. A dream. It was only a dream.

CUCKOO. It was real to me, lying here on the stones. My hands are sweating as if I had been fighting. For a moment I had forgotten where I was.

CUSACK. You remember me?

CUCKOO. The collector of truths.

CUSACK. The collector of lies.

CUCKOO. There is one I was keeping for another day. If I tell it to you now, will you give me my fee and ferry me across the Shannon so I can head for home? There should be a moon.

CUSACK. Why the hurry?

CUCKOO. I do not sleep easy in this monastery. The stones are too hard.

CUSACK. It is my bed every night.

CUCKOO. I have the best story of all but it is lying heavy on my brain. It would help me to discharge it, then I can think of God and his mercy.

CUSACK. Is it a tale of lechery? If so, you will have to wait until morning. I suffer enough in the night, alone, my hammer in my hand.

CUCKOO. It is not a story of that kind. Will you hear it?

CUSACK. As long as it is not a story of sleeping, birth or women.

CUCKOO. It is soon told. The men of Ulster saw a boy rowing over the sea towards the strand in a small boat. He had a pile of stones beside him and as he rowed with one hand, with the other he slung shots at the sea-birds, stunning but not killing them. When they had recovered he let them fly into the air again. The king, Conchobor, saw this and was impressed. He told the men of Ulster not to let the boy ashore as he was a worker of miracles. A warrior was sent out to stop the boy beaching his boat.

'Come no further,' the warrior said. 'What is your name?'

'I'll give my name to no man,' the boy replied. 'And you must get out of my way.'

'You can't land,' insisted the warrior.

'I'm going where I'm going,' said the boy. 'Even if you had the strength of a hundred men you would not stop me.'

With that he flung a stone. It roared like thunder and knocked the warrior headlong. So King Conchobor sent his greatest hero, Cuckoo.

'Name yourself or die,' he demanded.

'So be it,' said the boy and cut Cuckoo bald-headed with a stroke of precision.

'The joking has come to an end,' Cuckoo said. 'Now we must wrestle.'

'I'm too small. I can't reach up to your belt,' the boy complained.

So he climbed onto two standing stones and threw Cuckoo down three times. Then they went into the sea to drown each other and Cuckoo played foul by bringing to use his terrible barbed spear the *gael bolga* without the boy's agreement. He brought the bowels of the brave boy into a bunch around his ankles.

'You have hurt me badly,' the boy said.

'I have indeed,' Cuckoo said. He took the boy in his arms and carried him to where the men of Ulster were watching. 'I now recognise this as my own son,' Cuckoo grieved. 'Here you are. I have killed him for you.'

'Thank you,' said the men of Ulster. And they went home.

CUSACK. Here's your money. Keep it safe.

CUCKOO. You will remember the ferry over the Shannon. I'm sure there is a moon big enough for rowing a boat.

CUSACK. Take the boat yourself and leave it on the other side. Someone will need it from that direction soon enough.

The door of the cell is opened and closed. Pause. A bell sounds.

ALI (*waking*). Oh, what's that? What's that?

CUSACK. Quiet now. It's only the bell for vespers. (*Pause.*) When you get home, will you laugh at me, stuck here in this grave, outlining witless fantasies for the future generations?

ALI. Somebody has to do it. People won't always pass the truth from mouth to mouth. It will have to settle down, close its wings and be caught.

MAEVE. Brother monk, do you know what Maeve looked like? Has anyone ever described her to you?

CUSACK. Only half a picture has emerged, all her activities being concentrated below the waist.

MAEVE. Was she beautiful?

CUSACK. Well, here's what I've got about her so far. A tall, short, long-round-faced woman with soft-hard features and a head of yellow, black hair and two birds of gold upon her shoulder. She wore a cloak of purple folded about her body and five hands' breadth of gold across her back. She held an iron sword with a woman's grip over her head. A massive figure, so a little girl told me, something like her mother, no doubt. Probably a hunchback as well as a whore is my guess.

MAEVE. Many men loved her. That's good enough for me.

CUSACK. Go back to sleep now. You've a long walk home in the morning.

There is a knock on the door. It is opened.

CON. Cusack, my son, would you step out here for a moment? There is something I would like to discuss with you.

CUSACK. Yes, your Grace?

The door closes behind him. Change to the monastery general atmosphere.

CON. Are they all asleep in there?

CUSACK. Doing their best. Christian floors are hard.

CON. Cusack, my son, I have news. The exiled King of Leinster, Dermot McMurrough, has invited Henry the Second of England to invade Ireland to help him get back his throne. The English army has already landed.

CUSACK. And what do you expect me to do about it?

CON. Inform those people for me. I have a lot to do. We will have to adjust to the change.

CUSACK. With respect, they'll get mad.

CON. Not if it is properly explained to them. A papal bull has been issued supporting the English king's invasion.

CUSACK. Ah. They'll understand that.

CON. They will? Why so??

CUSACK. Because they'll find out that Pope Adrian the Fourth was once called Nicholas Breakspear, an Englishman.

The sound of alarm bells. Fade out the Clonmacnois general atmosphere. Sounds of battle. Fade. Fade in special atmosphere.

CUSACK. Good people, now you know how I have suffered — a man pickling fantasies like a grandma doing her onions. It was never my intention to get involved. All I wanted was a quiet life doing a simple job that I could understand.

Fade in the sound of rumbling inside the earth.

Instead, I had become amanuensis to Ireland's fighting heroes — head-hunters, cattle-farmers, violent dreamers, and, by writing them down, I had made them seethe and bubble under every age in Ireland like the earth's blood waiting to erupt and scald the sky.

The roar of a gusher. A long scream from CUCKOO.
Fade out special atmosphere.
Fade in abattoir atmosphere.

JANET (*crying*). Horrible, horrible! Clean it off me! I'm covered in it!

CUCKOO. Where are these bulls?

JANET. Stop it! Stop it!

CUCKOO. I'll balance them both on the point of my sword, skin them in mid-air, split them from nose to tail, scatter their bowels!

JANET. Stop it!

CON. Steady, Janet, steady. It's only blood . . . Just tell yourself, it's only blood. (*Pause.*) I'd consider it a favour if you'd let us wash the worst of this off.

MAEVE. Why? You look fine to me. Isn't red your colour?

JANET. This will never come out. My clothes are ruined. (*She weeps.*)

CON. Never mind, never mind. Don't cry now. Everything will be all right.

MAEVE. Do you know, I think these two are in love. Remember, Fergus?

FERGUS. With all my heart. Isn't your wife a great woman to love, Ali? What lucky men we've been.

ALI. Well, Fergus, you haven't had the pain with her that I have: this argument over equality.

MAEVE. That's true. Fergus has never doubted that I'm better than him. Which one of you meat-merchants is the stronger? In Ireland it's always the woman.

CUSACK. True, Maeve. The system was even exported to America.

The telephone rings.

CUSACK. That'll be news. It's all right, I'll get it.

MAEVE. When Ali and me were married we found that we were level-pegging in everything — power, position, possessions . . . nearly. We were a fraction out, so there was a furore. I'm a stickler for the final detail, you know.

ALI. A man less wise than your suffering husband might say that you were pedantic. We were equal down to our thumb-rings, our wash-pails, the rams of our flocks, the stallions for our horse-herds, but . . . I had a bull bigger and better than hers — Finnennbach, the white — and Maeve did not have the equal of him running with her cattle. There was only one other such bull in Ireland, in Cooley, Ulster.

MAEVE. I offered the farmer who owned it treasure, land, chariots, anything, and my friendly thighs on top of that. The fool said no.

ALI. So we had to go to war to match a pair of bulls. Where else would you hear such nonsense? Who cares about old and overblown cattle? Who wants them? We sold Ireland short with that war.

MAEVE. Oh, go on with you, it was good fun. Thousands upon thousands dead, all for the love of balance in nature. What do you say?

CON. Nothing, nothing at all.

FERGUS. It would never have happened if I'd had the taming of her, Ali. If I'd had Maeve from the beginning, as a young girl, what a woman I would have made of her. But now it's too late.

MAEVE. Wouldn't you do as much to be sure that you're getting your proper respect in the world?

JANET. Some of us do have to go to extremes to obtain that.

MAEVE. Ach, no one's equal now. They're just all as bad as each other. Don't you think so? I don't feel at home here.

CON. I think people are very confused now, you know, disorientated.

JANET. Yes. One big mess, isn't it?

MAEVE. No room for Cuckoo now. The childhood of Man is over. Bulls, battles, bravado . . . baloney. Nothing gets done for show any more.

JANET. Yes. No style left, no panache. It's all so mundane.

MAEVE. Is that so? So you think the world needs livening up a bit, do you? Why did you really come here this morning. Eh? We'll have the truth this time, if you don't mind.

CON. We were going out, together.

FERGUS. Into the fields. That was what I saw in the woman's black-ringed eyes. The fields. Flowers, birds. The good old fields.

CON. Yes . . . a picnic . . .

MAEVE. Ah, you were going to slip off and leave Cusack to it for the day? He said you had a habit of doing that.

ALI. Mr Sheehan, your clerk, of whom we have the highest opinion with the regard to the truth of his tongue, tells us that you often absent yourself for hours on end from your office, that your lunch takes from twelve till half-past three, in fact, that Cusack the clerk runs this place for you. Would that be a fair thing to say?

CON. No . . . I don't think so . . .

CUCKOO. So, you were going to feast in the fields?

CON. We were.

CUCKOO. After you'd eaten, there'd be some weapon play. Then you'd be at peace, lying in the grass, listening to the herds and flocks. She would be dreaming about children. He would be dreaming about cattle. If I was out there with you, I'd sit apart and dream of war. (*Pause*.) You're more of a warrior than he is, like Maeve. Set aside your shield. We'll have a little hand-to-hand.

JANET. Please, don't touch me.

CON. Could you see your way clear to stop doing that to her.

CUCKOO. I'd fight a thousand men at this ford. No one would cross. My feats of arms would amaze the armies. The river would run red. After that, we would lie in peace in the grass.

JANET. Don't touch me . . . please don't touch me . . .

CUCKOO. Once a woman and a fool were sent to trick me by Maeve. She thought that the man would not arouse my suspicions as he was idle, and the girl, Finnabair, would take my weapon. I cut off the woman's breasts and thrust a great stone pillar into her wound. The fool's few brains I knocked out then thrust another great stone pillar up his arse. These pillars still stand. They will always be remembered, Finnabair and the fool. Will you?

JANET. Why are you doing this to us?

MAEVE. There's nobody else around. Everyone is following the Pope.

JANET. We don't deserve it, you know. We've done nothing to upset you.

MAEVE. I don't know. You manage to get under my skin somehow.

JANET. We're ordinary people, for God's sake! Ordinary people! Aren't we, Con?

CON. Oh, yes. Very ordinary. Almost non-existent.

JANET. Can't you just do your sacrifice when the bulls come and leave us out of it? We'll just sit in the office or something until you've finished. We won't interfere, I promise.

CON. We'll keep out of the road, okay? You do as you like. Feel free. Make yourselves at home. Feel free.

The sound of running across the yard.

CUSACK. Would you believe it? Would you be able to throw your mind into such convulsions that you could find the angle to credit this I'm telling? In your greatest moment of faith and acceptance of the vicissitudes of life, would you be able to swallow this vicissitude? You take two points a hundred miles apart. One in Connaught, one in Ulster. You put a white bull in a lorry in Connaught and a brown bull in a lorry in Ulster, then you point them both towards Dublin. Are you with me? From entirely separate directions! A hundred miles apart. What are the chances that at a certain junction half-an-hour to the north-west of the appointed place, these two vehicles should take it into their heads to collide and the bulls to escape and go charging round the countryside?

FERGUS. Myself, I'd give that story no credence at all.

CUSACK. Right. Now struggle with the news that as I was talking on the telephone to the driver of one of these lorries I could hear the television going in the roadside cafe where the poor lunatic was licking his wounds and spending his hard-earned pennies on a call. The television programme was from Clonmacnois. I heard the commentator saying that the Pope was delayed, held up by all the heavy traffic in the sky. Every helicopter in Ireland is fluttering around him, getting in the way.

MAEVE. So we might still make it . . .

ALI. If they can recapture the bulls and get them here on time.

FERGUS. More delays can be expected. As soon as the great druid descends on the monastery there'll be thousands of children to kiss, hundreds of sacred places which cannot be passed without a prayer or a reverence. He'll be hugging the sick, giving blessings till his arm aches . . .

MAEVE. So, they're both late — the bulls and the Pope. He's held up in the sky. They're held up on the earth. Only destiny will bring them together at the right juncture, random fate. We're in the hands of Time itself.

CUCKOO (*thickly*). Where . . . are . . . the . . . bulls?

CUSACK. Any minute, Cuckoo . . .

CUCKOO. I can't hold back much longer. I'll have to fight something. All breezing around in my blood . . . battle-needs . . . I'm at the ford with my weapon . . . help me . . .

FERGUS. Quick, he's ready to blow. Get him something!

ALI. What? What can he hit here?

MAEVE. What have we got? All right, let him have these two for lack of anything better. Cuckoo! Here's a loving couple for you.

CUCKOO (*chanting*).
Slaughter, exile, corpses,
blood, ravens, wailing women,
heads bumping at my belt,
Bones smoking veins death
sings the Warped One! Death!
Beloved Death! Brother!

FERGUS. You don't mind helping out, do you? You're only going where thousands and thousands have been before.

CON. Look, I'd like to help, honestly . . . No! No! He doesn't want me!

CUCKOO. Is this all? It's not enough! A neck like that is nothing but a barley-stalk to slash with a stick. I must have . . . bulk! Bulk! Bulk!

CON. Don't hurt me . . . I'll find something . . . something he'll like . . .

ALI. You'd better be quick. He's on the verge of a major distortion.

CON. I'll get it, I'll get it . . . all right? He'll really enjoy this . . . stand back . . . where's my keys now . . . won't be long, now Cuckoo, I'm getting you fixed up . . . I've got something in the old fridge here.

A jangle of keys. The sound of locks and bolts as the doors of a freezer are opened.

ALI. Calm now, Cuckoo. They're getting you something to play with.

CUCKOO. Oooooh! Hurry up! I'm in terrible torment! Give me something to hack in mercy's name! Have you no pity? It's rising up in me . . . I can't hold on . . . I can't . . . Ha! I must hack and hew! Where . . . ? Where . . . ? A target! Wham!

CON. Gangway, there! Here it comes Cuckoo! Stand by! Solid meat.

The rattle and jangle of a beef carcass on a running rail. The clang of steel as CUCKOO *hits it with his sword.*

CUCKOO. Aaah! My hand! My hand!

ALI. What kind of trick was that to play on a man in torment?
Giving him a stone to hack at!

CON. It's frozen meat. If he'll give it time to thaw he can mangle it as
much as he likes . . .

CUCKOO. My hand is sprained. My elbow is absolutely dislocated.

MAEVE. The thing's as cold as ice. See, it steams but with winter. What
is it?

CON. It's a full carcase of beef.

MAEVE. Beef? What do you eat it with? A hammer?

CUCKOO. Is it Death? It's Death itself. Cold as the grave. Where's
the blood? Where's the bits of hair and fat? This was never alive. It's
a rock, a memorial pillar to some old hero I'm being taunted with
because I was never as good as him. (*To* CON:) My wrist will
remember that, when the sting's gone out of it . . .

JANET. You'd have killed me without a thought, wouldn't you?

FERGUS. He was in great need. It had to be let out.

JANET. You useless, gormless, revolting, layabout bastard!

She kicks him in the crutch. His body drops.

CUCKOO. Aaaaaah!

FERGUS. That must have been a good pamphlet.

JANET. Dirty, stupid lout! Disgusting, bloody moron!

CON. Janet, you really shouldn't have done that . . .

JANET. Oh shut up! I don't care now. Poking people about, they're
going to do this, going to do that. I'm sick of them. Bastard!

CUCKOO (*chanting*).
Now, broken and despairing,
brought low by a woman warrior,
I wish to die. My arm broken
by a dead bull, what hopes
of killing a live one?

CON. I'd like to apologise on her behalf. She's got this temper. It
doesn't often show itself . . . only under pressure, you understand.
She doesn't mean what she's saying.

CUSACK. The heroes find that hard to understand. Their lives were
all about consequences, Mr Sheehan. You did what you did, then
you stood up and took the racket, right on the jaw. You didn't
lie, or duck, when the axe came down.

JANET. Don't give me that! As soon as this place is surrounded you'll start negotiating for your miserable lives, and blaming everyone else for what you've done. That's what I loathe about you most. You can't accept consequences. If you kill then it's anyone's fault but yours. You're children, bloody children! I'm going.

MAEVE. Cuckoo, your admirer is leaving, so she says.

JANET. Come on, Con. We'll just walk out of here.

CON. Is that all right, everybody? (*Pause.*) Will you be able to manage, Cusack, old son! Lock up after you when you've gone.

MAEVE. So, you're off for your picnic?

CON. If it's all right with you. We won't mention this to anyone.

MAEVE. A drive in the country, a green field, a freshly laundered cloth laid out on the grass . . . Ah! You should have seen my armies at their picnics. Their dishes covered Ireland. (*Pause.*) If it weren't for the fact that you are about to offend against the holiest and most time-honoured law of all men, we might have let you go.

CON. What's that? Tell us and we'll sort it out.

MAEVE. Hospitality, Mr Sheehan, hospitality.

CON. Hospitality?

MAEVE. Look at us. We're starving. The last drink we had was hours ago. Our stomachs are rumbling. Our mouths are dry. You have no idea how far we've come.

CON. You want to share our picnic? Come on then, we'll all go.

MAEVE. No. We'll have it here. Janet, you go and get it. Mr Sheehan, Con to his friends, will wait with me.

JANET. What a vicious bitch you are.

MAEVE. Maybe, but I get even worse when I'm hungry.

JANET. What do you think, Con?

CON. Don't stand there making up your mind. Go and get it! Quick.

JANET. I think she's bluffing.

CON. Will you stop gabbing and do as they say?

JANET. Why should I feed them?

CUSACK. I thought it was your business to feed animals?

JANET. Not political animals.

MAEVE. Would you want we Irish to start eating each other? Surely not.

JANET. If I forget to say it when I come back — I hope it chokes you.

CUSACK. It doesn't look good for you, Mr Sheehan. Your woman has got impulsive and passionate about the state of her health.

CON. You won't forget to come back, will you, love?

JANET. Oh, stop snivelling, will you?

The door in the gate opens and bangs shut. Pause.

ALI. Do you have any doubts about her?

CON. None whatsoever.

ALI. Lucky man you are. Could I say the same, Maeve?

MAEVE. Oh, I'd come back for you, Ali.

FERGUS. And me, Maeve?

MAEVE. What have you got to offer, Fergus?

A car door slams. Pause. The engine starts.

CUSACK. Ah, perfidious Albion.

MAEVE. Well, it looks as though we've missed our picnic. Not that it's going to be one for you, Mr Meat-Merchant. Where do you want it? Head or heart?

CON. She's forgotten . . . don't . . .

MAEVE. Cuckoo, what will you give me to let you have the hacking off of this one's fat head?

CUCKOO. A chariot, a gold chain, two lengths of best purple cloth.

MAEVE. He's all yours but I think I got the best of the bargain.

CON. She thought the key to the ignition was the key to the boot. They're easily mixed up . . .

CUCKOO. Would you hold his head steady for me? He's bobbing about a lot.

CON. Or she might have left the picnic at home. She's got a head like a sieve . . .

FERGUS. Will you keep yours still and stop talking? There're certain forms to be observed in the taking of a head. The victim isn't expected to talk his way through the experience. Try a dignified and heroic silence.

CON. I'm sure Janet doesn't mean you to interpret what she's done as a sign that she's escaping. I think the woman is probably just turning the engine over to keep it supple . . .

CUCKOO (*chanting*).
What strength
in his brains,
what power,
in his blood,

what magic
in his marrow,
make mine.

ALI. Stick your neck out, man. Make things easier on yourself! Ready, Cuckoo?

CUCKOO. Oh yes! Oh, yes! Aaaaah!

CON. Would you pass on a message to my mother?

CUCKOO. Death! Brother! Embrace him!

The car engine is cut. A car door slams. Pause. The door in the gate opens and closes. The sound of footsteps which then stop. Pause.

JANET. Picnic time!

CUCKOO. Shit!

JANET. Everything has changed. We're on your side now. We believe you in everything you've said, don't we, Con?

CON. Er . . . yes . . . most definitely we do.

MAEVE. Not before time. We're getting impatient for our courtesy to be repaid.

CON. If you'll pardon my asking, what courtesy is that?

MAEVE. Do you think that we have ever doubted that you are what you are?

The sound of the picnic being laid out.

JANET. I think there's plenty to go round. We're happy to share it with you, aren't we, Con?

CON. Any barley loaves and small fishes? (*Pause.*) Sorry. Forget it. Oh, yes. There's plenty enough here, all right.

JANET. This is going to be great fun. I love picnics, don't you? Food just seems to taste better in the fresh air, I find.

MAEVE. Does it now? You taste all this, now. Everything.

CON. With pleasure. You're the guests. The best of service. Here we have bread. Cheese, Celery.

The sound of the crunching of celery.

JANET. Potato crisps.

The sound of potato crisps being crunched.

CON. Apples.

The crunching of apples.

CUCKOO (*over the sound*). Aaaah!

JANET. Roast beef. Mm. There. Is everything all right?

MAEVE. Some poisons take time to work.

CON. True. How do you feel, Janet?

JANET. Fine, never felt better. (*She burps.*) Ooops! Sorry.

MAEVE. If your food gives us the wind then the world will suffer for it. You know, don't you, Cusack? You've seen it yourself.

CUSACK. Hurricanes roar through the countryside and there's the noise of terrible thunder. Roofs get blown off houses. Whatever you do, Miss Soames, don't give them beans.

MAEVE. Have I got the head of the table?

JANET. Of course.

MAEVE. And I get served before anyone. Understand? I've had the legs of serving-men broken for forgetting that.

FERGUS. What's this?

JANET. A scotch egg.

FERGUS. It must be hard to be a hen over there.

CON. Tuck in. Would you be after having a gherkin, Cuckoo?

CUCKOO. Wha! Trophies from the small green giants.

ALI. And where were you going for your picnic, you two lovers?

JANET. We thought we'd go to Tara.

FERGUS. What does the likes of you want in Tara, the home of the high kings?

CON. Very into history, Fergus, old son. Fascinated. Not much is left there now but . . . the old vibrations . . . associations.

FERGUS. So this banquet was intended for Tara. The new high king and queen. Ireland ruled by meat merchants. This is good beef.

CUSACK. Prime quality, Fergus. The best. Know their meat do these two. Fresh, rare, succulent, young. Why shouldn't they take care of themselves?

MAEVE. I'm used to somebody singing my feed down. If I don't have music with my dinner I get trouble. Who is it worth asking?

CUSACK. C'mon, Mr Sheehan. Give Maeve a song.

CON. I don't know any songs, honestly. If I did I'd sing them for you.

ALI. Janet here strikes me as a singer; straight, bright like a bird, her eyes clear as rushing water. Sing to us, my love. Make a heartsore husband happy.

JANET. Well, I don't know really . . .

CUSACK. Now Miss Soames, isn't it true that you are an active member of the Anglo Irish Folksong Society?

JANET. How did you know that?

MAEVE. You have the look of a woman who can follow a tune.

JANET. Well, it's very difficult to just turn on a performance like a tap.

MAEVE. Cuckoo, in your experience, is it possible to torture a song from a human throat?

CUCKOO. Maeve, with these bare hands I have made a hundred heroes sing higher than larks and lower than moles.

CON. She'll sing, won't you, Janet? Come on now! We're waiting, dear. Give us a song, please.

JANET. Very well. I'll do my best.

She sings:

Of all the money that e'er I've spent
I've spent it in good company
And all the harm that I've ever done,
Alas, it was to none but me:
And all I've done
Through lack of wit,
To mem'ry now I can't recall,
So fill to me the parting glass,
Good night, and joy be with you all.

The heroes pick up the tune and harmonise with it, humming softly.
CUCKOO *whimpers tearfully.*

(*Sings:*)

If I had money, enough to spend,
And leisure time to sit awhile,
There is a fair maiden in this town
Who sorely does my heart beguile:
Her rosy cheeks,
And ruby lips,
I own she has my heart in thrall,
So fill to me the parting glass,
Good night, and joy be with you all.

The accompaniment gets stronger and sadder.
CUCKOO *cries.* JANET's *voice fades.*

(*Sings:*)

Of all the comrades that e're I had,
They were sorry for my going away,
And all the sweethearts that e're I had
Would wish me one more day to stay: door, Con, door

But since it falls
Unto my lot,
That I should rise and you will not, door!
I'll gently rise and softly call,
Good night and joy be with you all.

The door slams shut.

MAEVE. They're getting away, stop them!

A confusion of crockery. Rushing. Cries.

Poets and dreamers! Liars and minstrels!

Screams from JANET.

*The sound of running: a door is opened and crashes shut.
Outside in the street, the sounds of pursuit with shouts and cries.
Fade.*

MAEVE (*laughing*). What a pair! They never give up, do they?

CUSACK (*laughing*). They're not the only ones. I'm awestruck, totally.

MAEVE. People have been magnificent. Heart and soul.

CUSACK. And all off the cuff. Where do they get it from? I'm very impressed, I can tell you.

MAEVE. I thought Cuckoo was going to explode.

CUSACK. He frightens me, never mind them. But you, Maeve? Gorgeous!

MAEVE. Ach, go on with you.

CUSACK. I'm teeming with admiration. You've exceeded my wildest dreams. If I was a little bit younger . . .

MAEVE. Don't you mean older? I'm two thousand, remember?

Fade in uproar in the street. JANET *screams. The heroes laugh.*

CUSACK. Well, I think it's time we moved into the ultimate phase, Maeve. Put them right on the spot.

MAEVE. There's nothing else for it, is there? Here we go.

The sound of uproar at the gate. The door opens.

CON (*over the wall*). All right, all right, we were just checking the car . . .

Shouting, screaming, and the sounds of kicking coming into the yard. The door slams shut.

JANET. Get off you lousy bastards! Leave me alone! Kick them, Con! Kick them in the face like me! Stop it! Help! Bastards! Christ!

CON. Look, the car is on a parking meter. Parking meter . . .

MAEVE. Right. That's the last time we trust you two.

JANET. Oh, shut up, will you? Who cares? You're all bloody mad, all of you!

CON. Cusack, old son. You must help us. Early retirement, a reasonable pension, call in when you like for a cup of tea and a slab of sirloin big enough to cover the crossbar of your bicycle. I'm reading your mind now. The indignation of your friends about your treatment here . . .

CUSACK. Maeve, these bulls are not going to arrive on time, I'm afraid.

MAEVE. I think you're right, Cusack. We'll have to use these two for the sacrifice. It's a second choice but I suppose it's better than nothing.

CUSACK. With you all the way. Beggars can't be choosers. But what's the style of the sacrifice going to be?

MAEVE. I'm a one for disembowelling. Plenty of show.

CUCKOO. Or I could make holes so big that birds could pass in flight through their bodies with them watching.

MAEVE. I'm almost solid on disembowelling, then beheading.

FERGUS. What about the Hedgehog?

ALI. Oh, not that. I'm bored with the Hedgehog.

FERGUS. It's a great feat if done well. I've done a Hedgehog with thirty-seven spears in one man strung up like this, and I threw every one from a distance of five miles with a mountain in between.

ALI. Five miles, Fergus: Five miles?

FERGUS. All right then. You've caught me out lying. It was ten.

CUCKOO. How about the Bladder? I could do the Bladder for both of them. With one breath of mine down the throat of each I'd have them inflated to the size of . . . Ireland.

ALI. That's a great boast, Cuckoo. Do you mean each one to the size of Ireland, or both of them together to the size of Ireland?

CUCKOO (*Pause*). Both, I think.

MAEVE. That sounds the best to me. When we get the telephone call then you'll do the Bladder on both of them.

CUCKOO (*breathing deeply*). I'd better start stretching my lungs for this one. It will need plenty of puff to get these two hard cases up that big. I'd better start practising with the woman, I think. A little mouth to mouth . . .

JANET. Get off me!

CUCKOO. Ouch! She bit me!

ALI. You'd better try it first with the man, Cuckoo. He might go up easier.

JANET. If you kiss my Con I'll bite your balls off you thick mick bastard!

CON. Janet . . . calmly now . . . he can kiss me if he likes . . . it's only fun . . .

CUCKOO. You're doubting my strength, the truth of my boast. Now I've got a split lip I can't do the Bladder, so that's out, but there's the worst of the lot, Maeve.

ALI. Oh, no, not that . . .

FERGUS. Cuckoo, what a thought . . . not the . . .

CUCKOO. Yes . . .

MAEVE. The Sack of the Seven Entrances . . .

ALI. Whew! Dare we try it?

FERGUS. Come on! We've got nothing to lose. I'm for it. It's ages since I've seen that one done. It's a slow thing so let's start.

CUCKOO. Wham! Wham! Wham! Wham!

CON. Excuse me . . .

MAEVE. We've alighted on the right flower, us bees. That will be the kind of honey the gods will like licking. The Sack of the Seven Entrances.

CON. Excuse me . . . would you kindly tell . . . what exactly is the Sack of the Seven Entrances?

MAEVE. The Sack of the Seven Entrances? You don't know? And you up to your arse in folklore?

FERGUS. The human body is a sack with seven entrances. Count them. Nostrils. Ears. Mouth. Arsehole. Weapon or wound. Taking coin of the realm, the sack is filled to the brim with money from the seven entrances. I have seen it done only a couple of times. It takes so long that the skin of the victim goes green from the corrosion of the copper working in the bowels. The final pieces of silver tarnish grey in the nose and gold goes dull while blocking up the fundament, so to speak. Your man dies stiff with riches. (*Pause.*) Now, we'll be needing some coins.

CON. I've got plenty of change. Here.

A rattle of coins.

Come on Janet. Be helpful, dear. Swallowing coins, that's all.

The telephone rings.

CUSACK. That will be Clonmacnois. Everything's getting out of phase. Be with you in a minute.

Fade.

MAEVE. Where would you like us to start on the Sack with the Seven Entrances? The mouth I think, so they can't sing again.

FERGUS. I'll do the first one. A big silver coin. Is your mouth open, Con?

CON. You want me to swallow a coin? I'll swallow a coin.

CUCKOO. Fergus, the honour of the first stroke in this feat is mine. I claim it and I will not be crossed. Stand back before a better man.

FERGUS. The honour is mine! I claim it for myself!

CUCKOO. A death as ornate as this must belong to the higher hero. Me!

FERGUS. Let Maeve decide . . .

MAEVE. Ach, fight it out, fight it out. Give us some sport and spectacle. But no codding about, eh? The man killed is the man cured of pride.

CUCKOO. Fergus, my foster-father, no warrior holds you higher than me. I swear by Ulster's gods I'll churn you up like foam in a pool! I'll stand over you like a cat's tail erect! I'll batter you as easily as a loving woman slaps her son.

FERGUS. Cuckoo, my boy, it is with shame that I view the prospect of killing you. Now you won't see the great Sack of the Seven Entrances, or the shudder of the birth-pangs of a New Ireland. As druid and death come together in a cleaning. I taught you all I knew, with a few things I kept to myself. Those few things will kill you.

MAEVE. Hurry up. Fergus, if you are dying at any time soon, remember my friendly thighs. Will you dream to be buried there?

CUCKOO (*chanting*).
Old man, you will fall
at an heroic hand
which honours death
more than a son his father.

FERGUS (*chanting*).
The sun in a bold Ireland
will not shine brighter
than the blood of this boy.

CUCKOO. For the first coin, Fergus.

FERGUS. For the first coin, Cuckoo.

A crash of blades. Fade out abattoir atmosphere.

CUCKOO (*thinking*). His arm is raised. The way to his heart is opened.

A crash of blades in the abattoir atmosphere.
Fade out immediately.

FERGUS (*thinking*). His leg is too far forward for his weight . . . Thigh!

A crash of blades in the abattoir atmosphere.

CUCKOO (*thinking*). His shield's too low. A glimpse of his neck!

A crash of sword on shield in the abattoir atmosphere.
Fade out immediately.

FERGUS (*thinking*). He's unbalanced. A shove with my shield, a downward stroke to the head!

A crash of shield on shield, then sword on sword, then sword on shield in abattoir atmosphere.

CUCKOO. Ha! Grrr!

A crash of sword on sword, sword on shield, sword on sword. Pause.

FERGUS. Well done, Cuckoo. I taught you well.

CUCKOO. You're not too old to learn, Fergus.

FERGUS *laughs. Pause.*

MAEVE. What are you waiting for?

FERGUS. Our quarrel is finished.

MAEVE. To the death, I said.

FERGUS. I could have killed Cuckoo several times already.

CUCKOO. Yaaaah!

MAEVE. You're fooling yourself, Fergus.

FERGUS. I helped to bring the boy up!

MAEVE. By all the suffering gods of Ireland, if you do not fight I will kill you myself! What's left of you that's so worth keeping?

FERGUS. Maeve, I put the freedom of Ulster below the freedom of your heart. But now you have said enough. I see how you would be satisfied.

A crash of swords. Fade out abattoir atmosphere.

Thrust!

CUCKOO. Hack!

FERGUS. Swing!

CUCKOO. Cut!

FERGUS. Slash!

CUCKOO. Rrrrrrrrrrrrrrrip!

Fade in abattoir atmosphere. Fade out.

FERGUS (*screaming*). Aaaaaah! Blood.

CUCKOO. Guts.

FERGUS. Weak.

CUCKOO. Strangle.

FERGUS. Dying.

CUCKOO. Strangle!

FERGUS. Little knife.

Fade in abattoir atmosphere. Fade out.

CUCKOO (*screaming*). Aaaaaaah!

FERGUS. Thing I kept to myself. Dying. Wonder.

CUCKOO. My blood. Going. Lost. Death. Brother.

FERGUS. Brother.

Fade in abattoir atmosphere.

JANET (*screaming*). Oh, God . . . this is mad . . . mad! Can't you help them?

MAEVE. They're both dead. With honour, at least.

The rumbling of an earthquake; the clanking of steel.

CON. What's that? Is it me? Are you hearing things?

JANET. I'm going mad! Everything is moving! Stop it!

MAEVE. Mother Earth is trembling as she drinks!

The full force of the earthquake.
Screams from CON *and* JANET.

CUSACK (*his voice fading in over the end of the earthquake*). We did it! We did it! Pope John Paul is in my old cell! But how did we do it with no bulls?

MAEVE. Mother Earth wanted Cuckoo and Fergus. Look, it was their deaths which made the earthquake work.

ALI. At such a sacrifice, no wonder Ireland shook. (*Pause.*) It would never have worked with these two scrawny offerings.

CUSACK. Poor Cuckoo, poor Fergus. Well, Mr Sheehan, all we have to do now is wait for the tidal wave. Are you ready for it?

CON. How long have we got?

CUSACK. A matter of minutes.

Fade in the sound of lorries drawing up. The bawling of bulls.

JANET. What's that?

CUSACK. Would you credit it? It's the bulls arriving, I think.

The door opens.

CUSACK. Hold it, we'll get the gates open and then you can back in! Give the drivers a hand out there will you Maeve, Ali? Thanks.

The gates are opened.

JANET. But you don't need the bulls any more . . .

CUSACK. We can't send them all the way back now, can we?

CON. These are the two bulls of Ireland?

CUSACK. That's right.

CON. Thirty grown men can stand on the back of one of them?

CUSACK. Probably forty.

The sound of lorries backing in.

JANET. Keep them out of here!

The lorry engines cut. The sound of the bulls stamping and bawling.

CUSACK. Well, here's your consignment, Miss Soames.

JANET. I don't want them!

CUSACK. A deal is a deal. If you don't take these two old monsters then what will the dogs and cats of England do for dinner? If we all pitch in we might get their carcases down to the docks before the tidal wave sweeps Ireland clean. What do you say?

CON. I'd rather drown than look those two bulls in the eye. Leave them where they are!

CUSACK. Wouldn't you grant these two old Irish monsters a peaceful and humane conclusion? Shame on you! And, for the first time in their miserable, lecherous existences, the chance to be useful? Come on the white! Come on the brown!

The tailgate crashes down on the concrete loading ramp. The bulls' bawling and stamping rises to a crescendo, then cuts out abruptly. Booted feet march quickly down the lowered tailgate.

ALI. Good morning, Mr Sheehan.

CON. Ali? Is that you?

CUSACK. Let me introduce you to some heroes of the present: an inspector in the Irish Fraud Squad.

CON. Aaaah!

CUSACK. Who has been working hand in glove with a representative of the British Consumers Association.

MAEVE. Hello.

JANET. Maeve! No!

CUSACK. Ah, there's worse to come, Miss Soames. A stiff case of acute resurrection, I'm afraid.

CON. Fergus! You're dead! Cut to ribbons!

CUSACK. Not at all, at all. He's an official of the World Bank Agriculture and Animal Husbandry Division.

CUCKOO. Aaah . . . grrrr . . .

JANET. Oh, no! Not him! Not Cuckoo! Don't bring him back to life, please!

CUSACK. Don't worry, Miss Soames, he's only a member of the European Economic Community's Meat Products Standards and Subsidies Inspectorate.

CUCKOO. Grrrr!

CUSACK. I think.

CON. So! We're discovered!

JANET. Deceived and beguiled.

CUSACK. Within the convoluted and serpentine wickedness of the human mind would you think there resided sufficient diabolical skill and energy to invent an electrical meat-tenderising machine? As a further extension of this appalling concept — now working full-blast in an innocent-looking industrial building in Birmingham, invented and designed by . . .

CON. Me! I did it! Shame and humiliation! I want to be punished!

CUSACK. Would you further toss around in your reeling imaginations the improbable possibility that geriatric Irish cattle carcases are being shipped from Dublin to Holyhead on Monday mornings to feed this infernal machine? Would you care to haphazard a guess as to what company and what agent arranges this?

JANET. Who else but me? I fix it. I forge, fiddle and fantasise the paperwork!

CUSACK. Now sink deeper into shock and horror as your torment your brain-cells with the thought that reconstituted flesh from these ancient Hibernian herbivores is then sold at centres of the British meat trade such as Smithfield, posing as top-grade Irish beef.

CON. I've never been so ashamed in my life. How about you, Janet?

JANET. I'm full of self-disgust and remorse. I'm hoping for a very long prison sentence.

CON. By your brilliant subterfuge you have broken us down. We are both psychological wrecks, reeling under the impact of your ingenuity. Well done.

ALI. Thank you sir. We put a tremendous amount of hard work into catching you. You've no idea of the cost of all that special effects work we had to use. Can you imagine the price of an earthquake these days?

JANET. An excellent ploy, a dazzling piece of ethnic reconstruction which had us fooled all the way. May I add my congratulations?

ALI. Three months of research and rehearsal, it took us. Have you ever tried to learn Old Irish? Incredibly difficult. But none of it would have been possible without the help of your clerk, Cusack here, working for us on the inside.

CON. Yes, thanks Cusack, old son, thanks. Thanks a lot.

CUSACK. Just doing my duty, Mr Sheehan. You were robbing Ireland of her future. Without beef we'd be buggered.

CON. Thank heavens you stopped us in time then, before we could do too much damage. We will, of course, make a full confession.

ALI. Oh, good. That puts the crown on the whole scheme. I'm delighted. Thank you. Thank you.

CON. Think nothing of it. You deserve our fullest co-operation.

CUCKOO. Oooooh . . . aaah . . . grrrr . . .

ALI. Come on, snap out of it Cuckoo. Relax now. It's all over. The Black Maria won't be long.

CUCKOO. Is that it then? All over?

ALI. I'm afraid so.

CUCKOO. Grrr . . . I can't let go. . .

ALI. Look, you did a great job out there, but you must come back!

CUCKOO. No! I'm staying!

ALI. But they're expecting you in your office tomorrow.

CUCKOO. What office? What tomorrow? Help me, Cusack!

CUSACK. You're putting yourself in terrible danger, letting your mind be taken hostage by lies.

MAEVE. Open the book again!

CUSACK. Maeve! You as well? These lies are for the enjoyment of idiots, remember?

MAEVE. Start at the beginning.

CUSACK. What a terrible waste. All of you could have made something sensational out of your lives.

A hum.

CUCKOO. Quick, give it to us, give it to us, ooh, blood, slaughter, madness.

CUSACK. All right, all right. (*The opening of a book, the turning of pages.*) Once upon a time King Ali and Queen Maeve were in bed together arguing about equality.

Humming.

ALI. You were lucky to have married me.

MAEVE. Lucky enough was I on my own.

ALI. Think of the gifts I gave you.

MAEVE. Only three that mattered to me.

CON. And what might they be?

MAEVE. He swore never to be jealous, never to be mean and never to be afraid.

JANET. That's a tall order. Did he live up to it?

ALI. I didn't do too badly, did I, Fergus?

CUCKOO. Aaaa, that's better, that's better.

Fade abattoir atmosphere. Fade in music and Celtic twilight atmosphere. The heroes hum.

CUCKOO. All of Ireland to walk in. Life, death, blood, brother. Brother.

Fade.

Fade back Celtic twilight atmosphere. Maintain humming.

CUSACK. Good people, while they start at the beginning we'll have to make do with the end. One thought gives me comfort — you've got more sense than to be taken in by heroes of any kind. But I am actually eight hundred years old; so that when the police approached me to be their man on the inside and asked if I had any ideas as to how we might catch Con and Janet I was able to make a few suggestions which I thought might be appropriate to their transgressions. I can see from your ears that you believe every word I've said. With such a genial approval upon me, I'll take my leave. Good night.

Fade out the humming of the heroes.

THE DEAD IMAGE

by John P. Rooney

For Ann, Margaret, Aoife, Niamh and Mary Jo

John P. Rooney was born in Belfast in 1940 and, apart from four years in the mid-sixties spent in Australia, London and Dublin, has lived there ever since. Having begun his working life as an articled pupil in an architect's office, he continued this work and is at present employed in the design and supervision of public housing projects in Belfast's inner city areas. He is married and has four daughters.

His first writing success came when he had two television plays accepted by Radio Telefis Eireann; however, they were never produced. Radio Telefis Eireann did subsequently produce a radio play, *The Summer Madness,* which Rooney later rewrote for the BBC and which was produced on Afternoon Theatre in 1980. *The Dead Image* is his second play for the BBC. *The Queen's O'Neill,* an Irish historical play, was staged at the Arts Theatre, Belfast in 1980.

The Dead Image was first broadcast on BBC Radio 4 on 24th March 1981. The cast was as follows:

SAM	Liam Neeson
BILLY	Michael McKnight
WILLIAM	Joe McPartland
SAMUEL	Allan McClelland
MAN	Derek Halligan

Director: Robert Cooper

Fade up the sound of Lambeg Drums and artillery barrage.

The voices of BILLY *and* SAM *in an echoing ghostly acoustic.*

BILLY (*off*). Sam . . .?

Pause.

SAM (*off*). Billy?

Pause.

BILLY (*approaching*). Sam . . .?

Pause.

SAM (*approaching*). Billy . . .?

Pause.

BILLY (*nearer*). Sam?

Pause.

SAM (*nearer*). Billy . . .?

Cut to the distant thunder of continuous artillery barrage.

BILLY (*close*). Sam, yeh hoor . . .! Where were yeh?

SAM (*close*). Shsssssh . . . shut it!

BILLY. There's only five minutes. If the Major'd noticed you missin' . . .

SAM. Well he didn't did he!

BILLY. Shot for desertion you could'a been. Where were you?

SAM. Here . . . (*A rustle of paper.*)

BILLY (*amazed*). How did you . . .?

SAM. There's just a few mind. Don't let the others see.

BILLY. Ah . . . Jesus, mate . . .!

SAM. Swapped my canteen for them . . . a fella along the trench.

BILLY. You're a mad hoor!

SAM. I thought you could do with a smoke . . . look at the state of ye!

BILLY. I'll not forget this, mate . . .

A match being struck. Then a great relieved breathing out of smoke.

The oul' nerves needed a steadier . . .

SAM. You're not alone . . . Five minutes?

BILLY. Three . . . now.

SAM. When it stops.

BILLY. What?

SAM. When the barrage stops . . . we'll know.

BILLY. Oh Jesus!

SAM. Hey, Hey, Hey . . .! Take it easy!

BILLY. We'll stick together like old times, Sam . . . ay?

SAM. The oul' firm, Billy . . . sure we'll beat them wi' our caps.

BILLY. And we'll stick together?

SAM. Like I said . . . the oul' firm . . . Hey . . . Hey, what's the matter?

BILLY. Nothin'

SAM. It'll be a walkover, I'm tellin' ye.

BILLY. I'm all right.

SAM. Look . . . I'll go over the top first . . . right? You keep your eyes on me all the way across to Gerry's lines. I'm tellin' you . . . no sweat!

BILLY. I said I'm all right!

SAM. We'll show 'em what Ulstermen's made of . . . right oul' hand . . .

End sound effect of barrage . . . A whistle blows.

BILLY (*whispering*). 'O God our help in ages past . . .'

SAM. Come on . . . After me . . . (*Shouts.*) . . . No surrender . . . Yeahhhhhhhhhhh!

The sound of machine guns covers shouts and grows louder.

Cut to interior acoustic: 1981 — a small living-room.

WILLIAM. . . . And that's the last was ever seen or heard of them again, them two heroes wi' their Orange sashes streamin' behind them marchin' fearless into the German guns and vanishin' into the smoke of battle . . . (*Pause.*) Hey . . . you listenin'?

BILLY. Yeah . . .

WILLIAM. Well you can bloody try and look like it!

BILLY. Right da . . .

WILLIAM. You're a right cheeky pup got lately . . .

BILLY (*under breath*). Christ!

WILLIAM. It's mixin' wi' that Sam fella . . . I know it . . . He's the road
to no town, that fella, and, by God, you're as bad gettin'. To think
of your grandfathers, them two men who gave their all for King and
country in the flower of their youth . . . to think that the likes of
them could'a spawned the likes of you . . . It's beyond me!

BILLY. D'you ever give it a rest, Da?

WILLIAM (*stung*). Yeah pup yeah! You might be twenty but yer not
past gettin' a clout on the ear. Thank God, I'm man enough for that
yet!

BILLY. For Jesus's sake!

WILLIAM. Why aren't you marchin' wi yer lodge tonight . . . eh . . .?
eh . . .?

BILLY. I'm goin' round to Sam's.

WILLIAM (*disgusted*). I'm goin round to Sams' . . . You're never outta
that house! And what the two of yous is up to is anybody's guess.
Neither of you workin' and yet yis are never short of money for drink
and girls and flash suits . . .

BILLY. We've things to do.

WILLIAM. The first of July, the whole of East Belfast marchin' to
commemorate the Battle of the Somme, where my father, your
grandfather, gave his all . . . and you've got things to do . . . Do
you really care nothin' for the seed and generations that's gone
before ye . . .? Can it be true?

Look . . . wise up son . . . there's things in this life is sacred and
there's things is profane . . . and it's time you knowed the
difference . . . Hey . . . Hey . . . Where are you going? Stay there . . .
I'm talking to you . . . Hey . . .

The door slams. Cut.

*Sound effect from hallway of shrilling and drumming of Orange band
music outside. A door closes on the noise. A few footsteps are heard.*

BILLY (*calling*). Sam . . .

SAM (*off*). Kitchen!

Footsteps. A crunch of glass. The door opens.

BILLY. What happened to this?

SAM. Ah the photo. A bit of an accident. Did you meet my oul' fella on the way out . . .? He's off to meet your da in the pub?

BILLY. No. Your door was open though.

SAM. It's a wonder he stopped to open it the twist he was in.

BILLY. The usual?

SAM. Ach . . .

BILLY. I got it too.

SAM. The oul' bollix, it's all for themselves anyway. They never saw their own das . . . except in that bloody photograph there. That's why they're like they are . . . (*Tinkle of glass.*) What are you doin'?

BILLY (*off*). Just lookin'.

SAM. If I'd my way I'd a thrown it out years ago . . .

BILLY (*off*). There's a likeness there. I bet if we were in that old army gear we'd be the dead image of them.

SAM. Aw no . . . don't you start!

BILLY. . . . I always thought there was only the two of them, but look over here on the right almost off the photo . . .

SAM. . . . Oh aye . . .

BILLY. Strange we never noticed him before!

SAM. He's hardly Steve McQueen, is he?

BILLY. There's somethin' about that face though . . .

SAM. Nothin' that a head transplant couldn't put right.

BILLY. Do you get the feelin' . . . you've seen him somewhere?

SAM. I suppose . . . Here, that's snapshot hour over for this week . . . You brought the gear?

Sound effect of a tool hitting the floor.

BILLY. Two crowbars, hammer, two chisels, . . . oh aye . . . and a flask of tea in case we're a while at it . . .

SAM. You can leave that. Where we're goin' we'll not want to hang around too long . . .

BILLY. Did you have any luck with that job?

SAM. Aye . . . I didn't get it. Christ, they send you to some beauties . . . imagine me, a fully paid-up Prod, workin' as a security guard up in Andytown . . . I ask yeh!

BILLY. They eat their young up there.

SAM. Don't I know it! Here . . . let's get tonight's show on the road!

BILLY. Why tonight, Sam? Sure the streets is crammed. There's peelers everywhere . . . doesn't make sense . . .

SAM (*meaningful*). Aye . . . Our streets is crammed . . .

BILLY. Oh, no . . . ah, no, Sam . . . I'm not going over there! . . . No way!

SAM. But it's perfect, man! Look out the back window . . . all those streets over there with the doors and windows blocked up . . . it's deadsville . . . there's not a bloody sinner . . . and look at all that lead, all them flashin's round the chimneys and the stepped gables . . . The whole area's derelict . . . due for demolition . . .

BILLY. I don't need the money that badly . . . They play tig with hatchets over there.

SAM. Ach wise up, man . . . Even the peelers doesn't go in over there.

BILLY. You're forgettin' the army . . . I've seen them in and outta those houses . . . yesterday in fact . . . and the day before . . . honest Sam, its hairy! There's easier ways of gettin' yer kneecaps blown off . . .

Pause.

SAM. It's a ton each tonight.

BILLY. A hundred quid!

SAM. He's payin' the top rate, this fella.

BILLY. Jesus, Sam . . . that's some bread!

SAM. It's there for the takin, oul' hand.

BILLY (*weakening*). I don't know . . .

SAM. Look . . . you don't worry about the army . . . sure they're not interested in a couple of loyal Prods ekein' out their supplementary with a bit of lead thievin' . . . It's stuff they're lookin' for, bombs and guns and stuff . . . Them fellas won't bother us. Anyway there's been nothin' found over there for a year now . . .

BILLY. Aye, well the natives must be gettin' restless again . . . the army's been over there a lot this week . . .

SAM (*serious*). Look . . . this fellas givin' the top rate because I've promised him a regular supply . . . He's got to know I can deliver . . . right . . .? (*Appealing:*) Billy, you've gotta take a chance sometime . . . . . . are you on or not?

BILLY (*sullen*). I just don't reckon on goin' over there . . . that's all I've said.

SAM. Well, it's make your mind up time, isn't it!

BILLY. It's takin' a big chance . . . over there . . .

SAM (*tempting*). A hundred sheets oul' hand . . .! I've the van round the back . . . We could be in and out like a dose of salts . . .

BILLY. Yer a mad hoor . . . I've a feelin' I'll regret this.

SAM. No way . . .! Look . . . Ah, you can't see it now, it's too dark, but over there in all those streets of blocked up houses there's one house with a ground floor window unblocked. We can get in there, up onto the roof workin' our way along the street takin' the lead as we go . . . Simple!

BILLY. I hope you' right.

SAM. Aren't I always right? Now quit worryin' . . . let's get goin' before the oul' fella gets back from the pub . . .

Fade.

Bring up sound effect of a crowded pub.

SAMUEL. And he bloody threw it at me . . . his own father!

WILLIAM. Yer jokin' me Samuel!

SAMUEL. I'd hardly opened me mouth when he pulls the picture off the wall and fires it at me . . . In smithereens it is now!

WILLIAM. The wee get! Sure there's nothin' sacred these days.

SAMUEL. And him named after his granda.

WILLIAM. Sure my fella's as bad, for God's sake . . .

SAMUEL. Buck mad he was, William . . .

WILLIAM. The only things them fellas has inherited from their grandas is their names . . . and I'm afraid that's the height of it . . .

SAMUEL. Aye . . . Sam and Billy . . . two grand old names. We chose well.

WILLIAM. Plain but honest . . . Y'know Samuel, I don't hold with these modern fashions in names: Glen and Garry and the like. If you want a good name you needn't go past the Good Book . . . that's what I say.

SAMUEL (*cautious*). Ah . . . is Billy in the Bible, William?

WILLIAM (*indignant*). 'Is Billy in the Bible?' (*Thinks.*) Well if it's not it damn well ought to be . . . Here . . . Where do you suppose them two fellas of ours is now . . . eh?

SAMUEL. Drinkin', hoorin' . . . up to no good anyway . . . you can be sure of that.

WILLIAM. Where'd we go wrong . . .? I often ask myself that very question 'Where'd we go wrong?' . . . God knows I tried my best. I took him walkin' every Twelfth, every first of July, every Apprentice Boy's outing . . .

SAMUEL. 'And some seed fell upon stoney ground . . . '

WILLIAM. Aye . . . I think there you have it . . . there's a stone in the heart of those boys that wasn't in our generation or our fathers' generation . . .

SAMUEL. Them's true words . . .

WILLIAM. It doesn't come easy, talkin' like this about my own flesh and blood . . . y'understand? . . . but I've done all I can . . . there's no feelin' in the young ones these days, not like in our time . . .

SAMUEL. It's them not walkin' with the lodge that hurts most . . . it's like . . . a sort of insult to them that's gone before . . . y'know what I mean . . .

WILLIAM. There's times I try and tell him what it's all about . . . about the Somme and all, I might as well be talkin' to the wall!

SAMUEL. I know the feelin'.

WILLIAM. Unnatural . . . I call it . . .

SAMUEL. Unnatural . . . the very word! It's bloody unnatural for young fellas like that to care nothin' for their kin and country . . . (*Recites*.) 'Breathes there a man with soul so dead, who never unto himself hath said: "This is my own, my native land"?'

WILLIAM. Jesus, Samuel . . . that's lovely . . . lovely, that is! Is it from the Good Book?

SAMUEL. I . . . think so.

WILLIAM (*recites*). 'Who never unto himself hath said: "This is my own, my native land . . . This is my own native land . . . " '

Fade out.

Sound effect hard in on a crackle of machine guns. Panic breathing close to the microphone.

BILLY (*frantic*). Sam . . . Sam . . . down here! (*Close to.*)

The thump of a body hitting the ground.

. . . Jesus, Sam I thought you were a gonner . . . You said we'd stick together . . .

SAM (*struggling to speak*). Billy, Billy, thank God . . .!

BILLY (*hysterical*). You said we'd stick together, for Christ's sake . . . where were you . . . eh? As soon as we came outta the trenches you were gone . . . You left me . . . left me out there . . . I couldn't see a thing in that smoke . . . you said we'd stick together like always . . . It's murder out there . . . we're goin' to die, Sam . . . I know it . . . we're goin' to . . .

SAM. Billy, Billy! . . . I've been crawling on my belly for hours looking for you . . . It's bloody slaughter . . . all them Gerries was supposed to be dead after the barragge. A right cock-up this! You all right?

BILLY (*recovering*). . . . Sorry, Sam.

SAM. Bugger that . . . just keep cool. If you let yourself go out here, you'll really be done for . . . OK?

BILLY. Yeah.

SAM. We've gotta work somethin' out.

BILLY. Did you think it would be like this?

SAM. I wouldn't be here if I had, I'll tell you that!

BILLY. All those poor bastards lyin' out there. Did many of them reach Gerry's lines?

SAM. Through that fire? You must be jokin'. Them that isn't dead or wounded is hidin' in shell craters like this . . . runnin' straight into machine guns we were . . . madness.

BILLY. I wish I was back home.

SAM. Look, look . . . when I was crawlin' around out there I didn't look up too much, but when I did, I saw a sort of ruin of a house or somethin' just beyond the wire . . .

BILLY. Yeah . . . I saw that . . . all sorta blocked up except for one window . . .

SAM. That's it . . . Well if we can make it to there . . . it'll give us good cover till the next wave catches up with us . . . We better wait till it's dark, when Gerry can't see us . . . Hey . . . (*Pause.*) who's that . . . Over there . . .

BILLY (*off hand*). Oh, him . . .?

SAM. He's so covered in mud I could hardly make him out.

BILLY. Jumped in here just before you . . . Don't you recognise him? (*Pause.*)

SAM. His face is familiar.

BILLY. D'you not remember we used to fight with his crowd when we were kids . . .

SAM. Oh. . . . Aye . . .

BILLY. He's one of the other sort, y'know . . . from the other end of Lagan Row . . . down by the river . . .

SAM. Why doesn't he come over?

BILLY. Maybe it's our sashes. Maybe he remembers us.

SAM. Funny, us all bein' on the same side now.

BILLY (*bitter*). I'll never be on the same side as the likes of him.

SAM (*incredulous*). Ach . . . Come on, Billy!

BILLY. He was with us in trainin' . . . remember the eejit strayed into our photograph.

SAM. I have him now . . . I'll call him over.

BILLY. No.

SAM. No, what?

BILLY. I don't want him over.

SAM. You serious?

BILLY. I just don't want him over!

SAM. But we're all on the one side!

BILLY (*shouts*). I told you I'll never be on the same side as the likes of him . . .

SAM. Keep your voice down, can't you. He's heard you. And stop bloody glarin' at him . . . Jesus . . . this is rich . . . what's any of that matter out here . . .

BILLY. What are we wearin' these sashes for then . . . Do they mean nothin'?

SAM. Ach . . . for God's sake!

BILLY (*shouts*). Well they mean somethin' to me. I'm an Orangeman, and proud of it!

SAM. Sssssssshhh . . .

BILLY (*shouts*). I don't care who hears it.

SAM. See you . . . you'd start a row in an empty house, you would. We're all in the one boat . . . that's how I see it . . . and if you want to fight the Battle of the Boyne all over again . . . well . . . that's your affair. But I'm not . . . (*Shouts.*) Hey . . . mate . . . come over here . . .! (*Panic.*) Jesus, mate . . . don't go up there, stay here . . . For Christ's sake keep down . . . !

A crackle of machine gun fire close to.

SAM (*after a pause*). Jesus!

BILLY. The stupid bastard.

SAM. You and your bloody mouthin' . . . poor bugger must have thought we were goin' to shoot him, or somethin' . . . Jesus!

BILLY. Eejit!

SAM. Maybe, maybe his nerves were bad. Our whisperin' together and you shoutin' about your sash. (*Pause.*) Anyway, it doesn't matter now, does it.

BILLY. I didn't mean any harm.

SAM. Doesn't matter.

BILLY. What'll we do?

SAM. What do you mean?

BILLY. Will we bury him, or somethin'?

SAM. No need . . . look . . . the mud'll bury him.

Cut sound effect.

The sound of a van cruising uncertainly with much changing up and down of gears.

BILLY (*sourly*). In and out like a dose of salts, you said.

SAM. Give it a rest, can't you.

BILLY. Cruisin' around like this . . . somebody's bound to notice.

SAM. Can I help it if all the street lights is out. Didn't reckon on that, did I? . . . Bloody pitch out there . . . One street looks just like another.

BILLY. Let's go home, Sam.

SAM. Will you stop wettin' yerself . . . we'll be there soon . . . ah, ha! . . . here we are . . . see all these bricked-up houses . . . we're gettin' warm . . . Christ! . . .

A scream of brakes as a car stops. The sound of the engine running.

BILLY (*afraid, whispering*). Sam . . . what'll we do? There's about a dozen of them . . . Oh God!

SAM (*whispering*). Shut up! I'll do the talkin'!

MAN (*off*). Hold it there, fella!

SAM. Is there somethin' wrong?

MAN. I ask the questions. What's yer business round here?

SAM. We're deliverin' a TV . . . must'a taken a wrong turnin' somewhere. It all looks the same . . . the streets, like.

MAN. There's nobody to watch TV down these streets but the rats . . . You're not from around here, right?

SAM. No . . . Andytown. We're from Andytown . . . like I said: we're deliverin' a TV . . .

MAN (*suspicious*). Oh, aye . . . There's a lot of Oranges about today. (*Pause.*) What's yer name?

SAM. Seamus Flynn . . . and this here's my mate . . .

MAN. Let him speak for himself.

BILLY. O'Kane . . . Sean O'Kane.

MAN. Right. (*Pause*.) Seen any Brits about boys?

SAM. No.

MAN. A bit of advice. Don't hang about here . . . Could be dangerous when the Brits come round . . . Know what I mean?

SAM. Sure . . . sure. We want no trouble.

MAN. On yer way!

SAM. Right . . . right . . . thanks, boys . . !

The sound of an engine revving up and a vehicle driving off a little way.

SAM. Bastards . . . A right bunch of hoods, those!

BILLY (*excited*). I told you . . . I told you!

SAM. 'I told you . . . I told you.' You're goin' on like an oul' woman.

BILLY. Somebody's gotta have some sense. You knew we were takin' a helluva chance comin' over here . . .!

SAM. All right! All right! . . . We're OK aren't we . . . give it a rest.

Pause.

BILLY. I know yer man from somewhere.

SAM. Aye, I do too.

BILLY (*suddenly alarmed*). Where are you goin' . . .? You should'a turned left for home.

SAM. I'm not lettin' those bastards scare me off . . . There's a hundred quid there!

BILLY. You're goin' back?

SAM. It's OK . . . around the long way this time . . . they'll never see us.

BILLY. But you heard what they said . . . about the Brits . . . Wise up Sam!

SAM. Look, I'm tellin' you: the Brits aren't interested in the likes of us. Anyway why would they bother comin' down this way . . .? All these houses is blocked up except this one I told you about.

BILLY. I want'a go home, Sam.

SAM. We've come this far . . . I'm not goin' back now. We'll be there in a minute.

Pause.

BILLY. It's the photograph.

SAM. What are you on about?

BILLY. Yer man back there . . . where I've seen him before. He's the dead image of that fella . . . the one I showed you . . . on the old photograph . . .

Cut sound effect.

The sound of continuous gunfire in the background. Explosion.

SAM. Will you stay still!

BILLY (*struggling*). This wire . . . it was supposed to be cut!

SAM. Bloody artillery . . . Here . . . you're free. Look at those poor buggers hangin' there . . . Christ!

BILLY. We're gonna die, Sam!

SAM. Shut it! If we can just get to that house over there . . . come on . . . get movin'!

BILLY. I've never even fired a shot . . . just all day crawlin' over bodies, through wire.

SAM. Save yer breath . . . Crawl!

BILLY. Thanks Sam . . . for gettin' me outta that.

SAM. We're mates aren't we? Come on . . .

Cut sound effect.

The sound of a van cruising to a halt. Silence. Slamming of the van door. Silence.

SAM. Eerie, isn't it? Not a dicky bird.

BILLY. Come on . . . let's get in and get it over with!

SAM. Wait.

BILLY. Wait! What for?

SAM (*uneasy*). I don't know . . . it's just a feeling.

BILLY. I thought I was supposed to be the cautious one . . . Look there's nobody about . . . let's get the lead, and get home.

SAM. The house . . . it looks funny, doesn't it . . . with just that one big black hole where the window was . . .

BILLY. I'm killin' myself laughin' . . . let's go!

SAM. You can see where it had been bricked up . . . I suppose the army broke into it, searchin'!

BILLY (*impatient*). Look . . . are you comin' or not?

SAM. Right, right . . . keep yer hair on. I'm comin'.

Cut sound effects.

Inside the house. There is gunfire in the background. The scuffling of feet on a rubble-strewn floor.

BILLY. OK . . . there's nobody here. Relax.

SAM (*with a sigh of relief*). Great . . .! I'm glad to leave this lot off . . .! It's not much is it . . . not much roof left . . . but the walls will stop a bullet and that's all we want. Funny the Gerries didn't keep it for a machine gun post . . . seems ideal to me. Anyway, mustn't look a gifthorse in the mouth . . . Hey oul' hand . . . feelin' better now.

BILLY. God, Sam . . . I made a bloody fool of myself out there.

SAM. Don't worry about it. They say everybody cracks up at least once under fire . . . My turn's to come . . . Ahhhhhhhhhh!

A scampering noise.

SAM. . . . Jesus . . . what's that . . . ?

BILLY. Rats . . . euggggh!

SAM. Place is crawlin' with them . . . go on yeh wee buggers . . . (*Stomping noises.*) . . . Bugger off. Go on, bugger off.

BILLY. We can't stay down here . . . see if you can find the stairs . . . It'll be better above . . .

SAM. Hard to make out anything in this light . . .

Cut sound effects.

In a derelict house, 1981.

SAM. It's a right mess . . . There's winos come in here, I wouldn't be surprised . . . Wait a minute . . . hey look . . . tonight's paper.

BILLY. Sixth edition, that paper's only out about an hour. Somebody's just been in here . . .

SAM. Those hoods!

BILLY (*panicking*). God, it must be them . . . There's nobody else around, let's get outta here!

SAM. Now, hold yer horses . . . Look . . . think about it . . . they wouldn't be hidin' stuff in here, the only unblocked house in the street! Stands to sense . . . this'd be the first place the army would search . . . right?

BILLY. I don't like it, Sam.

SAM. Look . . . it's only the winos I'm tellin' ye. Will you get a grip!

BILLY. Let's get the lead and get home. (*Pause.*) Where's the stairs? It's hard to make out what you're walkin' over in this light . . .

Echo. Double-tracked voices.

SAM (*off*). They're over here . . . somewhere . . . Yes . . . here . . . I've got the banister . . .

Cut to heavy guns in the background.

BILLY. Go on for Christ's sake . . . the rats . . .!

SAM. Easy on . . .! Bloody dangerous this . . . There's treads missin'. Come you behind me.

BILLY. I'm here.

SAM. Easy now . . . come on . . .

The sound of feet ascending stairs. They stop.

BILLY. Go on.

Increasing double-tracking of voices to give the impression of two parallel scenes.

SAM. Wait!

BILLY. What?

SAM. There's a chair or somethin' wedged across . . .

BILLY. Can't you shift it?

SAM (*straining*). I'm bloody tryin' aren't I . . . Wait a minute . . . there's some wires holdin' it . . .

BILLY. Wires . . .! Jesus Sam . . . Noooooooooooooo!

Explosion.
Cut to double-tracked scream.
Cut to explosion/scream.
Cut. Silence.

Fade up external acoustic. Funeral. A helicopter hovers in the distance.

SAMUEL. A nice touch that: buryin' them together like . . . a fittin' touch!

WILLIAM. Sure weren't they inseparable them two . . . like you an' me, oul' han', and like our fathers before us . . . Ah . . . but . . . sure it's the end of the line now, no mistake . . . the end of the line . . .

SAMUEL. They said it was meant for the soldiers.

WILLIAM. Who gives a damn what them murderin' hoors say . . . (*Conspiratorial.*) You heard the news this morning?

SAMUEL. Yer man?

WILLIAM. Aye . . . down by the river they found him . . . with his head sawn off. The murderin' bastard . . . he'll not harm any of ours again, that's for sure!

SAMUEL. It was quick work that.

WILLIAM. Aye . . . and our boys'll rest the quieter for it . . . Blood for blood . . . that's the only way to finish it. That's the way we've always finished it.

Fade down exterior acoustic.

BILLY (*calling as at the beginning*). Sam?

SAM. Bill?

BILLY (*fading*). Sam?

SAM (*fading*). Bill?

Lambeg Drums cross-faded over sound effects.

THE BIGGEST SANDCASTLE IN THE WORLD

by Paul Thain

For my father

Paul Thain was born in South Shields in 1949. He has a degree in Drama and Theatre Arts from Birmingham University. He recently gave up his job teaching English in a London Comprehensive in order to write full-time. He has since written several plays for radio. He lives in Norfolk with his wife and daughter.

The Biggest Sandcastle in the World was first broadcast on BBC Radio 4 on 23rd December 1981. The cast was as follows:

ARCHIE	Colin Douglas
TOMMY	Geoffrey Matthews
JIMMY	John Hollis
BETTY/JOYCE	Kathleen Helme
MICK	James Bate
HARRY/HAMISH	Christopher Fairbank
FRED	Brett Margolis
ARTHUR	Gordon Faith
JACKIE	Fred Pearson
HIGGINS	Trevor Cooper
EMPLOYMENT OFFICER/NEWSCASTER	George Parsons
REPORTER/MP	David Gooderson
TV DIRECTOR	David McAlister

Director: Glyn Dearman

Fade in beach sounds. Waves break, seagulls mew; dogs bark.
In the distance is the sound of children playing. A cold wind blows.

    Fade to an afternoon interior in a workingmen's club. It is
    Tyneside 1981.

JIMMY (*putting his glass down*). Did A ever tell you aboot one of the
   most marvellous days of me life?

TOMMY. Naw?

JIMMY. A'm bein' serious now.

ARCHIE. This should be good.

JIMMY. Aye, it is. Now listen . . . It was the first time A went on the
   ferry . . .

TOMMY. . . . the ferry . . .?

JIMMY. Aye. The *old* ferry . . . Not the fancy new one. (*Pause.*) It was
   when A was a bairn . . . A must have been aboot seven. Me Mam was
   takin' me to Whitley Bay, you see . . . Oh . . . it was bloody
   marvellous. A'd get meself lifted up, so's A could luck doon int'
   engine-room . . . All smoke an' steam, it was . . . (*He chuckles.*) A
   used t'think it was on fire, an' that we'd all droon . . . Anyroad . . .
   there was these two blokes down there you see, stripped t' the waist
   . . . shuvellin' coal by the ton . . . A tell you, Tommy . . . the sweat o'
   those two men would shove that ferry from one side o' the Tyne t'
   the other . . . a dozen times a shift . . . Oh hey . . . But the engine
   itself . . . Why, man . . . A'd never seen anythin' so powerful . . .

   Pause.

TOMMY. Haven't been to Whitley Bay for years.

ARCHIE. Is that it then?

JIMMY. What?

ARCHIE. Your story . . .

JIMMY. Aw . . . naw . . . that was just the beginning that was. You
see, after we'd had our fish an' chips, we went an' sat on the beach.
But the thing was, you see . . . they was havin' this sandcastle
competition. So while me Mam was havin' a quiet sleep, A got
crackin' with me bucket an' spade. An' when A'd finished . . . Why,
man . . . you should've seen it . . . Was A proud . . .!

TOMMY. Did you win?

JIMMY. Win what?

TOMMY. The competition. For your sandcastle.

JIMMY. Naw . . . A was very nearly highly recommended, mind.

ARCHIE. Oh, aye?

JIMMY. Aye . . . If it hadn't been for that dog peein' on me turret
just before the judge arrived . . . Still . . . it didn't matter . . . it was
more the sense of achievement, you know?

ARCHIE. Aye, A do.

TOMMY. Happy days, eh?

JIMMY (*wistfully*). . . . Aye . . . (*Pause.*) Well, it's my round, A think . . .

ARCHIE. Aw . . . Save your money, man . . .

JIMMY. Now what's it for, Archie if not to spend, eh?

TOMMY. That redundancy money'll not last forever . . .

JIMMY. A'll worry aboot that when it happens. (*He gets up.*) Same
again, is it?

ARCHIE. Just hold your horses. We've all afternoon yet. You can't just
sit an' get half-cut everyday, you know, Jimmy . . .

TOMMY. Archie's right.

ARCHIE. Surely there must be somethin' more constructive than —

JIMMY. Well, like what? Like go lookin' for a job?

ARCHIE. Listen . . . A'm not talkin' aboot that . . .

JIMMY. Well, A certainly am. The only constructive thing A want is a
job . . .

ARCHIE (*sighing*). How old are you, Jimmy?

JIMMY. Fifty-one. Just gone.

ARCHIE. Well, then . . . face facts, man . . . None of us sittin' here is
ever likely t' work again.

JIMMY. You never know . . . A mate o' Tommy's got a start, just the
other week. An' he was nearly as old as me. That's right, Tommy?

TOMMY. Aye, but . . . he was skilled.

ARCHIE. You see . . . there's just no demand for plain muscle these days. Not that you've got a lot of that left.

JIMMY. Oh, you think, d'you? Well, there's still a good day's work left in me Archie . . . Make no mistake aboot that. A could show you a thing or two, A could . . .

ARCHIE. You reckon, d'you?

JIMMY. A do. Not much chance o' puttin' it to the test though, is there?

ARCHIE. Oh, A don't know . . . just 'cos you're not bein' paid, doesn't mean it's not work.

TOMMY. Watch it, Jimmy . . . he'll be havin' you diggin' his garden . . .

ARCHIE. No, no . . . Jimmy's given me a much better idea than that . . . Not so much a competition . . . more of a challenge.

Fade sound effects.

Fade up kitchen sounds. It is a few hours later. There is a clatter of dishes. ARCHIE *is helping his wife,* BETTY, *with the washing-up.*

BETTY. You're goin' t' do what?

ARCHIE. Look, Betty . . . How many more times . . . ?

BETTY. You must be goin' daft, or somethin' . . .

ARCHIE. Mebbe.

BETTY. But, Archie . . . you're a grown man . . . sandcastles is for bairns . . .

ARCHIE. Not the one we're goin' t' build . . . it'll be the greatest sandcastle you've ever seen. The size of a hoose . . . bigger even . . .

BETTY. Well, A know how bored an' . . . an' . . . depressed you've been gettin' . . . but . . . well . . . don't you think you should have a word wi' Doctor Mallard . . .? He's got some tablets that cheer you up.

ARCHIE. A don't want any bloody tablets.

BETTY. Only Peggy was sayin' just the other day . . . her Alf's got some . . . and the' seem t' work wonders. He's champion now. Just sits quietly in his garden all day.

ARCHIE. You can save your breath. Me mind's made up. Don't you see? A've just got to have somethin' to occupy meself . . .

BETTY. A know you have, pet . . . And A know A'm always goin' on about you findin' an interest, but —

ARCHIE. Betty . . .

BETTY. But what're people goin' t' think, Archie?

ARCHIE. They can think what the' like . . . If a grown man can spend half his day chuckin' darts . . . or watchin' football . . . A don't see what can be so potty aboot buildin' a sandcastle.

BETTY. Hmph!

A final crash of a plate. Fade sound effects.

Fade in the sounds of the beach. It is early the following morning. Waves crash restlessly; a single gull cries in the distance.

ARCHIE. Right, Jimmy.

JIMMY. Shouldn't we wait for Tommy?

ARCHIE. Naw . . . it's too cold to hang aboot. A want t' get crackin' . . .

JIMMY. So . . . How do w' start?

ARCHIE. Why, first we'll mark oot a full-scale plan. Like the architects do. Leave your bucket wi' me and . . . d'you see that rock yonder . . .?

JIMMY. Only just.

ARCHIE. Aye, well . . . walk towards it, an' cut a line. A straight line, mind . . . with your spade . . . A'll tell you when t'stop. Go on, then . . .

JIMMY. Here, Archie . . . what aboot the tide? You sure we're far enough up?

ARCHIE. Aye.

Throughout the following, JIMMY *is moving further and further off, marking a line in the sand with a spade.*

JIMMY. Well as long as you're sure . . . only A can remember waves comin' right up to the cliffs . . .

ARCHIE. . . . Once in a blue moon . . . That's right . . . Keep it straight . . .

JIMMY (*off*). You know . . . our lass thinks A'm crackers . . .

ARCHIE. Aye . . . mine does too . . .

JIMMY (*off*). A reckon Tommy might've had second thoughts . . .

ARCHIE. Don't you worry. He'll turn up. Got nowt else t' do, has he?

JIMMY (*off*). Here. How much further?

ARCHIE. Till A tell you.

JIMMY (*off*). Bloody hell . . . it's goin' to take up half the beach . . .

ARCHIE. That's the idea . . . right . . . you can stop there.

JIMMY *stops.*

Now . . . Turn a right angle . . .

JIMMY (*off*). You what?

ARCHIE. A right angle. Turn a right angle. No, no . . . the other way . . . Now. A'll cut a line with you . . . parallel like . . . Now just see you keep it straight . . . We don't want a crooked perimeter.

JIMMY. No. I know. (*He starts to mark a line in the sand with his spade.*)

ARCHIE. This is where the battlements are goin' t' go, you see . . . with a turret at each corner.

JIMMY (*off: making a parallel line*). Oh, aye?

ARCHIE. We'll make the walls wi' the sand w' dig from the moat. If w' dig deep enough, the sand should be nice an' damp, so's w' can shape it better . . .

JIMMY (*off*). . . . shape it . . .?

ARCHIE. Oh, aye . . . Nothing too fancy, mind . . . but w' can learn as w' go along . . .

JIMMY (*off*). You've got it all worked oot, haven't you?

ARCHIE. Why, just the basic idea . . . then we'll have ourselves a canny size courtyard, with a keep in the middle . . .

JIMMY (*off*). A what?

ARCHIE. A keep. Where the baron would live.

JIMMY (*off*). Oh, A see . . . A say, Archie . . .?

ARCHIE. What now? A said watch your line, man.

JIMMY (*off*). A'm tryin', A'm tryin' . . . What was A sayin' now? Oh, aye . . . A don't suppose w' could get into any trouble for this?

ARCHIE. What? For building a sandcastle?

JIMMY (*off*). Aye, A know it's a sandcastle, but . . . it isn't goin' to be just any —

ARCHIE. — Diven't worry, man. (*He stops the line.*) Right. That'll do. Stop there. Now turn another right angle —

JIMMY. — Oh, not another one!

ARCHIE. — 'an meet up wi' me.

JIMMY (*starting to approach, marking his line with his spade*). Here, there's Tommy now.

ARCHIE. Told you he'd turn up, didn't A? Careful wi' that spade. You're goin' a bit wonky . . .

TOMMY *approaches across the sand.*

TOMMY. Lovely mornin' . . . Bit nippy, mind.

ARCHIE. Bit o' work'll soon cure you o' that.

JIMMY (*closer*). Mind where you're standin', Tommy. That's our perimeter. For the battlements.

TOMMY. Oh . . . sorry . . .

ARCHIE. Sleep in, did you?

TOMMY. Naw . . . A didn't as it happens. That's where you're wrong. A've been doon t' the library.

ARCHIE. Oh, aye?

JIMMY. Can't you afford your own newspaper, then?

TOMMY. No need for sarcasm, Jimmy. Just so happens A was doin' some . . . er . . . research . . .

ARCHIE. Research?

TOMMY. Aye. On sandcastles. You know . . . the best way t' go aboot it . . .

ARCHIE. . . . And . . .?

TOMMY. Well . . . bit disappointin' really . . . They didn't seem to have much at all . . . In fact, they had nothin' . . .

ARCHIE. You sound surprised.

TOMMY. Why, there was plenty on proper castles, mind. You know . . . ones made o' stone. But, nevertheless, they were very helpful. Nice young lass . . . even looked up the Guiness Book O' Records . . . But there was nowt there, either . . .

JIMMY (*arriving and ceasing his line marking*). What? Nothin' at all? D'you mean there's no world record?

TOMMY. Mustn't be . . .

JIMMY. . . . But don't you see? Can't you see, Archie? We could go doon in history . . . This is our chance, man . . . world record holders . . . Just think o' that . . .

ARCHIE. Well, don't get too excited, Jimmy. We've hardly started yet.

TOMMY. It's goin' t' be a canny size, mind.

JIMMY. Aye, it is . . . the biggest in the world . . .

ARCHIE. Right, then, you two . . . Let's see what sort o' workers you really are . . .

Fade sound effects.

Fade up beach sounds. It is a few hours later. The mechanical chomp of a spade slicing through sand is counterpointed by the natural rhythm of the waves. Two small children approach.

FRED (*approaching*). What y' doin', mister?

ARCHIE. An' who might you be?

FRED. Me name's Fred.

ARCHIE. Is it now? An' does your friend have a name, Fred?

FRED. Her name's Joyce. An' she's not me friend. She's me sister.

ARCHIE. A see. Can't she be both?

JOYCE. Why you diggin' such a big hole, mister?

ARCHIE. Well . . . Can you keep a secret?

FRED. Aye.

ARCHIE. An' what aboot you, Joyce?

FRED. She can an' all . . .

ARCHIE. Well, listen here, then . . . Do you know what pirates are . . .?

FRED.
JOYCE. · · · Aye . . .?

ARCHIE. Well, we're three o' them. And d'you see that man standin'
on top that geet big pile o' sand . . .?

FRED. Aye . . .?

ARCHIE. Well, they call him Peg-leg Jimmy. You might have heard o'
him . . .?

FRED. Naw . . .

JOYCE. Are you havin' us on, mister?

ARCHIE. Now, naw . . . It's true A tell you. Hey . . .! Peg-leg Jimmy . . .!

JIMMY (*distant*). . . . You what . . .?

ARCHIE. Aye you, you daft bugger. Come an' drag yourself ower
here . . .! . . . The thing is, you see, he's got such a terrible memory . . .
even forgets his name sometimes. But worse than that . . . he's
forgotten where he buried our treasure. And that's what we're looking
for.

JIMMY (*approaching*). What's all this aboot then?

JOYCE. Show us your leg, mister.

JIMMY. Eh . . .?

ARCHIE. Oh . . . he won't show it to anyone . . . bit embarrassed he
is. Aren't you?

JIMMY. Archie, would you mind tellin' me --

ARCHIE. -- Your peg-leg, man. Where that crocodile bit you . . .

JIMMY. . . . Oh . . . Oh, aye that . . .

ARCHIE. Told you he had a terrible memory, didn't A?

FRED. Where's your ship then?

ARCHIE. Oh, we left that in the river . . . in case we were followed . . .

TOMMY (*distant*). . . . Hey . . . you two . . .! Am A expected t' do all this work on me own . . .?

ARCHIE. Aw . . . diven't fret, man . . . Why don't you make yourself useful an' pour the tea . . . Flask's in me bag.

FRED. Here, mister . . . can we help you look for the treasure . . .

ARCHIE. Oh, not here you can't . . . Tommy the Tartar ower there . . . He's our Captain, you see . . . an' he might get a bit upset . . . A'll tell you what, though . . . A reckon Peg-leg might've buried it over there . . . behind that rock . . .

JIMMY. Oh, aye . . . A certainly could have done . . .

ARCHIE. Don't say A said anythin', mind.

FRED. We won't.

The sound of feet as the children move off.

FRED (*calling*). An' don't forget . . . We'll want a share . . .

TOMMY (*approaching with mugs of tea*). Here you are lads . . . it's a bit stewed, A'm afraid . . .

JIMMY. Always is oot of a flask.

TOMMY. What did them bairns want?

JIMMY. Archie told them we were pirates . . . lookin' for buried treasure . . .

TOMMY. . . . Oh, aye . . .?

They all chuckle. Pause.

JIMMY. Why . . . A don't know aboot you two, but A'm feelin' a bit knackered . . .

ARCHIE. Aw . . . you soon get used to it again.

TOMMY. A remember when A was labourin' on the buildin' sites . . . You'd always be laid-off just before Christmas . . . you know . . . For a few months till the weather got better . . . But the first day back . . . My God . . . it was awful . . . You'd ache all over . . .

ARCHIE. Aye . . . and then you'd worry yoursel half t' death wonderin' when the job would end . . .

TOMMY. Aye.

JIMMY. Archie . . .?

ARCHIE. Aye?

JIMMY. A was thinkin' aboot this drawbridge . . .

ARCHIE. Aw . . . Jimmy, man . . .

JIMMY. Naw, naw . . . Let me have me piece . . . A realise we can't make it go up an' doon . . . but if we were t' lay driftwood across the moat, we could cover it wi' sand . . . and then we could have the water runnin' all the way round . . . like a proper moat . . .

TOMMY. Good idea, Jimmy . . . An' A think A saw some planks further up the beach . . .

Four or five unemployed TEENAGERS *approach, led by* MICK *and* HARRY. *They chant.*

TEENAGERS. How-way the lads. (*Clap-clap.*) How-way the lads. (*Clap-clap.*)

MICK. What y' doin', Grandad . . .? Diggin' yourself a grave?

HARRY. A think you'd better hurry . . . You don't look as if you've got long left.

JIMMY. . . . You cheeky young monkey . . .

ARCHIE. Leave him, Jimmy . . . He's only a kid . . .

HARRY. A'm old enough, mister.

ARCHIE. Are you? Well why don't you act it, then? Show a bit o' respect . . .

MICK. . . . Bit o' respect . . . What . . .? For three dirty old tramps . . .?

JIMMY. Hey, A'll warm your lug for you in a minute . . .

TOMMY. These happen t' be oor workin' clothes . . .

MICK. . . . Workin' clothes . . .? Hey, did you hear that lads? A think they must all be waitin' for Guy Fawkes Night.

The TEENAGERS *laugh.*

TOMMY. An A think *you* must be sick o' livin' . . .

MICK. Oh . . . threats, threats . . . eh, Harry? You're gettin' us really scared . . .

HARRY. We just want to know what you're doin', that's all.

JIMMY. Well, we're buildin' a sandcastle.

ARCHIE. Right. You've been told. Now bugger off.

HARRY. Buildin' a sandcastle . . .!

MICK. Hey, man, they're a bunch o' loonies. Probably escaped from some funny farm . . .

JIMMY. Right. That does it.

HARRY. Oh . . . watch him, Mick . . . he's turnin' violent. Goin' all red aboot the face, he is.

The TEENAGERS *laugh.*

MICK. Come on then, Grandad . . . Show us how you did it in the old days. Oh . . . the old left hook, is it? Come on then . . .

JIMMY. Right!

The smack of a punch to the face.

MICK. Ow . . .! That hurt!

JIMMY. Aye . . . an' there's another one where that came from an' all . . .

TOMMY. Aw . . . it's not worth it, Jimmy.

JIMMY. No . . . Go on . . . Get the hell away, while you still can.

MICK (*moving off*). You'll regret that, mister . . . Bloody loonies. They ought t' have you locked up . . . loonies . . . bloody loonies . . .

HARRY (*moving off like a monkey*). . . . Ugh, ugh, ugh, ugh . . .

The TEENAGERS *all join in, ad libbing, they go. Pause.*

TOMMY (*sighing*). . . . A don't know what gets into kids these days. A don't.

ARCHIE. A seem to remember you were a bit of a lad yourself, Tommy . . .

TOMMY. Aye . . . A know . . . But not like that, Archie. Things have changed, man . . . an' certainly not for the better either . . .

ARCHIE. Aye . . . mebbe . . . But it's not all their fault, is it? A mean, they've just got nowt t' do wi' themselves . . . Same as us . . . Only it's worse really . . . A mean . . . Don't you remember how you felt when you got your first pay packet?

TOMMY. Oh, aye, A do . . . vividly . . . A was heartbroken . . . Me mother took most of it . . .!

ARCHIE. Aye, an' quite right too . . . But it helped you feel grown-up, didn't it? I mean, feel a bit important. An' that's what them kids haven't got.

JIMMY. Aye, well . . . We'll not get finished bletherin' all day . . .

TOMMY. That turret o' yours is lookin' good, Jimmy.

JIMMY. Aye . . . it's comin' on . . . A seem to have a talent for it . . . A thought A might get meself a block o' marble . . . an' a nice young nude model . . . (*He laughs.*)

ARCHIE. Get your missus t' pose for you . . .

JIMMY. Oh . . . dear me Archie . . . A'd need an awful lot o' marble . . . about ten ton!

They all laugh. Fade sound effects.

Fade in sound effects of a living-room a few hours later. BETTY *is sitting watching the news on television.*

NEWSCASTER. '. . . helping police with their enquiries. And there's also some good news on the jobs front . . .'

The back door slams.

BETTY. That you, Archie?

NEWSCASTER. '. . . A defence contract, worth over two hundred million pounds, will bring nearly seven hundred new jobs to the ailing North.'

BETTY *switches off the television.* ARCHIE *enters the living-room.*

ARCHIE (*approaching*). Who else you expectin' . . .?

BETTY. My . . . you look jiggered . . .

ARCHIE (*sitting in his armchair*). . . . A feel it . . . pet.

BETTY. Well, your supper's on . . . Be ready in a minute . . . Toad in the hole . . .

ARCHIE. Champion.

BETTY. So how's it goin' . . .?

ARCHIE. Oh, it's comin' on . . . Tommy an' Jimmy are real good workers when the' set their minds to it. Where's the paper?

BETTY. Under the cushion. (*Pause.*) Archie?

ARCHIE. Aye?

BETTY. A'm sorry about what A said last night.

ARCHIE. You've no need to be pet.

BETTY. . . . It's just that A was . . . you know . . . a bit taken aback . . . Surprised, that's all . . . A mean . . . It did seem a bit . . . a bit pointless . . .

ARCHIE. That shouldn't have surprised you . . . Most things A've done seem a bit pointless . . .

BETTY (*reproachfully*). . . . Now, Archie . . .

ARCHIE. Aw, come on, pet . . . You know as well as A do, that it's true . . .

BETTY. Well . . . We cannot all go down in the history books, you know . . .

ARCHIE. Mebbe not. But that wasn't me meanin' . . .

BETTY. . . . A don't know, Archie . . . Still . . . if it's making you happy, that's all that matters, isn't it?

Clean out sound effects.

Fade in the sounds of the beach. It is early morning, the next day. The mood to be established is one of cold, grey melancholy. The waves now seem tired, dragging back small stones and pebbles as they lethargically repeat their cycle. A single, bass-register fog-horn sounds far in the distance. A solitary gull cries plaintively.

JIMMY (*after a pause*). Oh, dear, dear me . . . Just look at that . . . Me bonny turret . . . All of a pile.

TOMMY. What aboot my battlements? Tumbled into the moat. Now who would dae a thing like that?

ARCHIE. Probably one of them kids Jimmy clouted yesterday.

TOMMY. But where's the sense in it, Archie?

ARCHIE. Aye, well . . . No use cryin' over split sand, eh? Won't take long t' put right.

JIMMY. But the same thing'll just happen again.

ARCHIE. Not if we're here t' stop it, it won't.

JIMMY. What? You mean all through the neet?

ARCHIE. An' why not? In pairs o' course . . . For the company. You can bring your fishin' line, Tommy. Catch us a few flatties for breakfast.

TOMMY. Aye, why not? We can collect some driftwood. Build oursels a fire to keep warm.

JIMMY. God knows what my Elsie'll say . . .

TOMMY. Aye? Who's the man in your hoose, then?

JIMMY. Aye, A know aboot that, Tommy. But standin' guard ootside a bloody sandcastle . . . Mebee them kids was right . . . They will be puttin' us in a looney bin.

ARCHIE. Jimmy Redpath! Have you come here t' talk, or t' work?

JIMMY. Aye, all right, man. There's no need t' go on. A get enough o' that at home.

Fade sound effects.

Fade in sounds of the beach. It is midday. The 'mood' has changed. The foghorn has stopped. The waves no longer sound oppressive. Children laugh and play in the distance. JIMMY *is singing while re-building his turret.*

JIMMY. 'Wor Geordie's lost his penka,
Wor Geordie's lost his penka . . .'

TOMMY *joins in.*

JIMMY.   'Wor Geordie's lost his penka,
TOMMY. Doon the double raa . . .'

ARCHIE *joins in from off.*

JIMMY.   'Cos he dropped it doon the cundy,
TOMMY.   He dropped it doon the cundy,
ARCHIE.   He dropped it doon the cundy,
                  Doon the double raa . . .'

JIMMY (*solo*).
      'So he went an' fetched a claes-prop,
      He went an' fetched — '

The REPORTER *approaches.*

REPORTER. Excuse me. Do you mind if I ask what you're doing?

JIMMY. Ask away, bonny lad. But A should've thought it was pretty obvious.

REPORTER. Er, yes . . . perhaps I should have asked why, rather than what.

JIMMY. Oh, well . . . that's a different matter. You see that fella ower there, by them battlements . . . cuttin' the slit windas?

REPORTER. Yes.

JIMMY. Well, he'll tell you. Call him 'Archie.'

REPORTER. Thanks.

JIMMY. What you want t' know for, anyway?

REPORTER. Just curious . . . All part of the job, really. I'm a journalist, you see . . . with the *Chronicle.*

JIMMY. Getaway . . .? Archie . . .!

ARCHIE (*distant*). What?

JIMMY. This lad here's from the papers. Wants a word with you . . .

ARCHIE.. . . Does he now . . .?

Fade sound effects.

Fade in sounds of the living-room. It is evening. There is a rustling of a newspaper from off.

BETTY (*entering excitedly*). Archie! Archie! You're in the papers . . . All of you are. They've even got your photo . . .

ARCHIE. Let's have a look.

A rustling of the newspaper.

BETTY. There . . . I think it looks wonderful, Archie. Like out of a fairytale . . . An' just look at your faces . . . Grinnin' like bairns . . .

ARCHIE. Give over, lass . . . Never mind that . . . What does it say?

A rustling of the newspaper.

BETTY. Ee, Archie . . . It's got that you're unemployed . . .

ARCHIE. Well I am, aren't A? No shame in that.

BETTY. Aye, A know, love but . . . But you don't want the whole world t' know . . .

ARCHIE. Don't A? Don't A just.

Clean out sound effects.

Fade in sound effects of the beach. It is that evening. JIMMY *stands by* TOMMY *who is fishing. The crackling fire counterpoints the gently lapping waves.*

JIMMY. It's a bonny night for fishing, Tommy.

TOMMY. Aye . . . It is that, Jimmy.

JIMMY. Just look at all them stars . . . hundreds of them . . . thoosands even . . .

TOMMY. What? Why, there's millions up there, man.

JIMMY. Getaway . . .

TOMMY. It's true A tell you.

Pause.

JIMMY. Hey, 'you think, Tommy . . . there might be a couple o' lads somewhere up there . . . lookin' doon here . . . wonderin' if there's a couple o' lads like us lookin' up there . . . wonderin' the same thing . . .?

TOMMY. Eh?

JIMMY. A said . . . D'you think that . . . Oh . . . it doesn't matter . . .

The bell on TOMMY's *rod rings.*

That sounds like our breakfast. Reel the bugger in.

Clean out sound effects.

The sounds of the living-room that same evening.

BETTY (*incredulously*). . . . You're goin' where . . .?

ARCHIE. A've told you. Doon t' the beach.

BETTY. But it's nearly ten o'clock, Archie . . .

ARCHIE. A know. An' A'll be late relievin' Jimmy if A don't get a move on. Where's that paper?

BETTY. Never mind the paper. You'll catch your death standin' on that beach all night.

ARCHIE. A'm well wrapped up an' we've got a big fire goin' . . . Look pet . . . It's not for long . . .

The telephone rings in the hall — off.

ARCHIE. Can you get it, love . . .?

BETTY *gets up with a sigh.*

ARCHIE. Ah . . . There it is . . . You were sittin' on it . . .

The telephone is picked up off. There is a rustle of paper as ARCHIE *picks it up.*

BETTY (*off*). . . . Archie . . . There's a man wants t' speak t' you . . . He says he's from the BBC . . .

Clean out sound effects.

Fade in sound effects of the beach the same evening. A fire crackles.

JIMMY. . . . D'you mean t' tell me . . . thoosands of years ago . . . we all crawled oot of that sea . . .?

TOMMY. Aye . . . that's right . . .

JIMMY. Wi' no clothes on . . .?

TOMMY. Naw . . . we weren't like we are now, man. We were like lizards.

JIMMY. Lizards?

TOMMY. That's right. Lizards.

JIMMY. Getaway . . . So then what happened?

TOMMY. Well . . . we sort of . . . evolved . . .

JIMMY. Evolved? But A always thought w' came from monkeys?

TOMMY. Why, we did. But that wasn't till much later.

JIMMY. A think A'd better hoi some more wood on that fire . . . (*He does so and the fire spits and crackles more.*) Can't beat a good fire, can you? A've always loved the crackle and splutter of a fire . . .

ARCHIE (*approaching*). Catch owt?

TOMMY. Oh, hello, Archie . . . Aye, we've got a couple . . .

ARCHIE. Champion. Any trouble?

TOMMY. Naw . . . nowt. A think they're only brave when there's no one aboot . . .

ARCHIE. Aye . . .

JIMMY. 'Ere, Archie . . .?

ARCHIE. Aye?

JIMMY. Did you know . . . accordin' t' Tommy here . . . that you were once a lizard . . . ?

ARCHIE. Eh? Aw, never mind aboot that . . . Here . . . feast your eyes on that.

A rustle of the newspaper.

JIMMY. What's this then?

ARCHIE. An' A've somethin' even better t' tell you both an' all.

Quick fade of sound effects.

Fade in the sounds of the beach. It is the following morning. An occasional gull mews. Children play in the background.

EMPLOYMENT OFFICER. Excuse me . . .

ARCHIE (*slightly off*). What now?

TOMMY (*slightly off*). Not another one . . .

EMPLOYMENT OFFICER. Excuse me . . . Mr Booth, Redpath and Sugden? I'm from the Department of Employment.

TOMMY. Congratulations.

EMPLOYMENT OFFICER. The thing is —

JIMMY (*approaching*). Who's this then? You're not the lad from the telly, are you?

ARCHIE. He's from the dole . . .

JIMMY. Is he now? Found us all jobs, have you?

EMPLOYMENT OFFICER. Er, no . . . I'm sorry . . . I —

JIMMY. — Naw . . . Didn't think you had somehow . . .

ARCHIE. What's it all aboot then, son?

EMPLOYMENT OFFICER. Well . . . it's about this . . . er . . . sandcastle, actually . . . We . . . er . . . read about it in the *Chronicle* last night . . .

JIMMY. And you've come to see for yourself, have you? Isn't it grand? Could be a world beater, that . . .

EMPLOYMENT OFFICER. Yes, yes . . . it's very . . . er . . . impressive. The thing is though . . . If you continue here, then, strictly speaking . . . you're not really available for work . . .

ARCHIE. . . . Not available . . ? 'Course we're available . . . We've been available for nearly three years . . . What you talkin' aboot?

EMPLOYMENT OFFICER. The National Insurance Act of 1948, and its subsequent amendments . . .

ARCHIE. Listen, son . . . It's very nice of you t' come all this way t' tell us this, but . . . you know . . .

EMPLOYMENT OFFICER. . . . It is a grey area, I must admit, but . . .

JIMMY. Grey area . . .? What's this lad on aboot, Tommy? A can't make head nor tail . . .

EMPLOYMENT OFFICER. You see . . . really you should still be out looking for work . . .

TOMMY. Looking for work! Aw . . . Give over, man . . . You think we haven't tried . . .? There is none. Not for the likes of us, anyroad . . .

JIMMY. You just don't know you're born, son.

EMPLOYMENT OFFICER. Yes, well . . . I'm afraid I've been told to tell you that we may have to stop your benefit if you . . .

ARCHIE. You what?

EMPLOYMENT OFFICER. Stop payment of benefit . . . Under Section —

ARCHIE. — Bloody hell . . .! You've got a nerve, haven't you?

JIMMY. Now here —

EMPLOYMENT OFFICER. — The case will have to be examined by —

JIMMY. Aw . . . dear me . . .

EMPLOYMENT OFFICER. There is, of course, an appeals procedure . . .

ARCHIE. Listen, bonny lad . . . One of us is crackers, and A'm pretty sure it's not me . . .

EMPLOYMENT OFFICER. Look. You don't think I enjoy this, do you? I'm just trying to do my job.

TOMMY. Haddaway to hell, man . . .

EMPLOYMENT OFFICER. Well, I'm afraid that's the law . . .

ARCHIE. Is it now?

JIMMY. If it weren't for the likes of us, you wouldn't have a job. Now what d'you think aboot that?

TOMMY. You tell him, Jimmy.

JIMMY. A will.

EMPLOYMENT OFFICER (*moving off*). Yes, well . . . There's obviously no point in my standing here —

ARCHIE. That's the first sensible thing you've said, son. (*He calls after him.*) An' you can tell your gaffer . . . he knows where he can put his dole money . . .

Pause.

JIMMY. Here, Archie . . . Can they really do that?

ARCHIE. Sounds that way.

TOMMY. Eh . . . Makes you think, doesn't it? . . .? A mean . . . What d'they expect us t' do all day?

ARCHIE. Aye, A know.

TOMMY. A mean . . . How do they expect you to keep some dignity, if they carry on like that?

ARCHIE. Why . . . like he said . . . he's just doin' his job . . .

TOMMY. But they make you feel so terrible, man.

JIMMY. A know what we should have done . . . We should've dug a dungeon an' hoi-ed the bugger in it . . .

They laugh.

Hey up . . . Looks like the people from the telly . . .

Quick fade of sound effects.

Fade in beach sounds again. It is a few minutes later. The DIRECTOR *is briefing* HAMISH, *his cameraman.*

DIRECTOR. Now Hamish . . . I'd like a nice, smooth panning shot from the sea . . . along the line of the cliffs . . . then coming to rest on the sandcastle itself. Okay?

HAMISH. Yeh.

DIRECTOR. Then I'd like you to pan gently from the moat . . . along the battlements . . . over the drawbridge . . . and up towards the keep. Okay?

HAMISH. Yeh.

DIRECTOR. It seems to be clouding over a bit . . . No problem with light, is there?

HAMISH. No.

DIRECTOR. Fine. Good. Er . . . er, Mr Booth . . .?

ARCHIE (*off*). Aye?

DIRECTOR. I'd like a few shots of you and your friends standing on top of the castle, if that's all right?

ARCHIE (*off*). Fine by me. Jimmy! Tommy! Get yoursels over here.

DIRECTOR. Oh, and Hamish . . . Did we . . . er . . . manage to get hold of that Union Jack?

HAMISH. Yeh . . . Debbie's got it . . .

DIRECTOR. Smashing. (*He moves off slightly.*) Mr Booth . . .? Ah, good . . . Thank you, Debbie . . . Mr Booth . . . I'd like one of you to be holding this . . . You know . . . Waving it high above the head . . .

ARCHIE (*slightly off*). What for?

DIRECTOR (*slightly off*). Oh . . . you know . . . flying the flag . . . An Englishman's castle, and all that . . . the viewers'll love it.

ARCHIE (*slightly off*). A see.

JIMMY (*slightly off*). Oh, can A do that, Archie? It'll be just like that Davey Crockett film. You know . . . The one aboot the Alamo . . .?

ARCHIE (*slightly off*). Go on, then.

TOMMY (*slightly off*). Your chance o' fame at last, eh, Jimmy?

DIRECTOR (*approaching*). Okay, Hamish . . . How does that look?

HAMISH. If the one on the left could just move a little closer . . .

DIRECTOR. . . . Mr Booth . . .?

TOMMY (*slightly off*). Jimmy! Watch what you're daeing with that flag. You nearly poked me eye oot.

DIRECTOR. Mr Booth . . . If you could just move a little closer . . .

HAMISH. That's fine.

DIRECTOR. Smashing. Right, Hamish. Turn over.

The camera whirrs.

DIRECTOR. Start waving the flag please, Mr Redpath . . .

ARCHIE (*slightly off*). Jimmy, man . . . Be careful . . . You'll have it all tumblin' doon.

JIMMY (*slightly off*). A'm actin', man . . .

TOMMY (*slightly off*). Aye, well . . . Act a bit more slowly, can you?

Pause. The camera continues to whirr.

DIRECTOR. That's great. Fine.

The camera stops.

DIRECTOR. All right, Hamish?

HAMISH. Yeh.

DIRECTOR. Okay . . . er . . . gentlemen . . . Thank you . . . That was marvellous . . . You can come down now . . . I'd just like a short interview . . . Which one of you's going to be spokesman?

JIMMY (*slightly off*). You're the man, Archie . . .

Quick fade of sound effects.

Fade up beach sounds. It is a few minutes later. ARCHIE *is being interviewed. A camera whirrs softly.*

DIRECTOR. Mr Booth . . . The creation of this enormous sandcastle has been seen by some as a potent symbol of protest . . . directed against the Government's attitude to the unemployed. What do you have to say about that?

ARCHIE. Well . . . A wouldn't know really . . . It was just that we were gettin' so bored sittin' around all day. You see . . . the thing is . . . We've all of us been grafters since we left school. And, you know . . . when we lost our jobs . . . Well, we haven't been, you know . . . educated to do anythin' else, really, you see. That's the top an' the bottom of it.

DIRECTOR. So you're not blaming the Government?

ARCHIE. Why, A'm not sure who you can blame. Not really. A mean . . . It's a different world now, isn't it? Everythin's changin' . . . an' so fast . . . You know . . . what with all these robots an' computers . . . Naw . . . but it's really the kids that's just leavin' school A feel sorry for. It's them that's goin' t' have the real problems.

DIRECTOR. Mr Redpath tells me you're hoping to establish some sort of world record?

ARCHIE. Well, if we do, we do . . . But that isn't the important thing. A mean . . . you've just got to keep yourself busy, haven't you?

DIRECTOR. Well, you've certainly been doing that. To have dug so much sand, in such a short time, must be quite an achievement?

We hear the distant approach of a bulldozer.

ARCHIE. Why, that's nowt that, man. When me father was down the mines, he'd have to shovel ten ton o' coal in a single shift. And that was bendin' doon all the time. Workin' on his hands an' knees . . .

The bulldozer draws closer.

JIMMY. 'Ere, Tommy. What's that doing here?

TOMMY. A bulldozer . . . a bloody bulldozer . . .

DIRECTOR. Hamish, make sure you get all this.

JIMMY. Bulldozer? What would they want that for?

ARCHIE. Can't you guess?

JIMMY. What? Me bonny sandcastle? They can't do that.

ARCHIE. Can't they just.

TOMMY. You see that one carryin' the briefcase?

ARCHIE. Aye.

TOMMY. Well A know that bugger. Call him Arthur Ridley . . . Used t' be inspector o' works for the cooncil . . . Before they stopped buildin' hooses, that is . . .

ARCHIE. Aye, A've heard of him.

JIMMY. But what w' goin' t' do?

ARCHIE. Well . . . Now that we're so close to finishin' . . . If they want t' knock it doon . . . They're goin' to have to drive that bugger over me first . . . Are you with me?

TOMMY. . . . A'm with you, Archie . . .

JIMMY. Well, if you're sure . . .

ARCHIE. Oh, A'm sure all right . . . Come on . . . Make a straight line and keep close together . . . We'll meet them head on . . . Right then . . .

They walk towards the on-coming bulldozer.

JIMMY. Here, Archie . . . What if it doesn't stop?

ARCHIE. You're not goin' to be frightened off by a machine, are you?

JIMMY. Well, no . . . but . . . But, A mean . . . it's a bloody big one, isn't it? Not exactly what you'd call a dinky toy . . . A'm not that sick o' livin', you know . . .

TOMMY. Aw, stop your frettin', Jimmy. Let's see a bit o' backbone, eh?

The bulldozer stops.

ARTHUR (*off*). Hey you men. . . . Get oot the way! A said . . . Get oot the way . . .! Are you deaf, or summat . . .? A said . . . Are you . . .? Higgins . . .! Switch that bloody thing off, will you . . . A can't hear meself think . . .

The bulldozer engine dies.

ARTHUR (*approaching*). That's better. Now. My name's Arthur Ridley. And A'm from the cooncil . . .

ARCHIE. Oh, aye?

ARTHUR. A see now you've got the bloody television cameras here . . . Gettin' your faces in the papers wasn't good enough, eh?

DIRECTOR (*approaching*). Er . . . Mr Ridley . . . I wonder if you'd mind —

ARTHUR. No bloody comment . . . Now bugger off . . . This is a private, municipal matter . . . It's got nowt t' do with you people . . .

DIRECTOR. I'd simply like to . . .

ARTHUR. A said . . . bugger off . . . now. What's all this daft carry on aboot, then?

ARCHIE. None of your business, that's what.

ARTHUR. None of my business . . . Oh, dear me . . . You'll make a laughin' stock o' the whole bloody town, man . . .

ARCHIE. How's that?

ARTHUR. How's that? How's that? A'll tell you how's that . . . Just think on what happened to Jarrow . . . That march was fifty years ago . . . And *still* people remember . . . Now what sort of municipal image is that over there, eh?

ARCHIE. It's just a bloody sandcastle, man . . .

ARTHUR. Look. A know you can't be expected to understand what they call public relations . . . but take my word for it . . . the Mayor's goin' potty . . .

TOMMY. A'm surprised you can tell . . .

ARTHUR. Oh . . . A see . . . Like that is it . . .? A might have known . . . A bunch of bloody troublemakers, eh? Well, I have instructions here . . . direct from the borough surveyor . . . to knock that bloody thing doon . . .

ARCHIE. Not while A'm here you won't . . . It's not doin' any harm . . .

ARTHUR. It's a public menace, that is . . . Just look at the size of that moat . . .

ARCHIE. That'll be all right . . . We're goin' t' flood it when we're finished . . . for the bairns t' swim in . . .

ARTHUR. *That* is a danger to the public . . . an' if you don't —

ARCHIE. — What aboot them cliffs, then? Aren't they a danger? Are you goin' t' knock those doon as well, are you?

ARTHUR. Them cliffs are a natural resource . . . and as such . . . are protected . . . But as to that . . . that . . . monstrosity . . .

JIMMY. Now here —

ARTHUR. I must advise you . . . that under the Town an' Country Plannin' Acts —

ARCHIE. You what?

ARTHUR. An' since you have not got plannin' permission —

ARCHIE. Are you daft, or summat?

ARTHUR. Oh . . . what's the use . . .? A should know better than to appeal to reason. Higgins! Knock that bloody thing doon!

HIGGINS (*off*). Oh . . . A don't know aboot that, Mr Ridley . . .

ARTHUR. I beg your pardon?

HIGGINS (*off*). Well . . . You never said nowt about any sandcastle . . .

ARTHUR. You get paid to work . . . not to think, Higgins. Do me out of a job, would you?

HIGGINS (*off*). Naw . . . A'm sorry . . . A can't do it . . . Not after all the work them lads've put in : . . It wouldn't be right . . . A think you'd better get someone else.

ARTHUR. . . . . Do you realise what you're sayin' . . .?

HIGGINS (*off*). Oh, A do, Mr Ridley . . . A'll tell you what A will do, though . . . A don't mind usin' me bulldozer to help them finish it . . . Get done in half the time . . .

ARTHUR. What?

ARCHIE. No thanks, mate . . . It's very nice of you, but we started this by hand, an' that's the way we want t' finish it . . .

JIMMY. Hey, look! Archie! Tommy! There's Jackie wi' some o' the lads . . .

TOMMY. Aye . . . an' all carryin' buckets an' spades . . .

JACKIE (*approaching*). Hey up . . . What's goin' on here, then?

ARCHIE. It's all right now, Jackie . . .

JACKIE. It better be an' all . . . Here . . . Am A goin' to be on the telly?

JIMMY. You never know.

JACKIE. Getaway . . . Wait till A tell wor lass . . . Who's that fella? The daft lookin' one wi' the fancy briefcase?

ARTHUR. I heard that.

JIMMY. He's from the cooncil.

JACKIE. Is he now?

ARTHUR. Yes. Yes I am. And if you don't mind . . . Some of us have a job t' do . . . Higgins! Was that your final decision?

HIGGINS (*off*). It was.

ARTHUR. Well get oot o' that cab, then . . . A'll do it meself . . .

JACKIE. You'll have to fettle with us first . . .

HIGGINS (*off*). If you get into this cab, Mr Ridley . . . I promise you . . . my union'll have somethin' t' say . . .

ARTHUR. My God! Is it any wonder the country's in such a mess . . . Come on, Higgins . . . Back to the depot . . . (*He moves off.*) You men haven't heard the last of this. You mark my words.

JACKIE. Bugger off.

JIMMY. Aye . . . an' good riddance.

HIGGINS (*slightly off*). Oh . . . He's not as bad as he might seem. Believe me . . . A've known worse . . .

ARTHUR (*off*). Higgins!

HIGGINS (*slightly off*). Well . . . A'd better be away . . . A might bring the bairns down t' see your castle after work . . . if that's all right?

ARCHIE. You'd be welcome.

HIGGINS *revs up his bulldozer and leaves.*

JACKIE. My . . . That's a canny castle you've got there, Archie . . .

ARCHIE. Aye, it is that.

JACKIE. We thought you might need a hand . . .?

ARCHIE. Aw . . . That's very good of you all . . . But we want t' finish it ourselves . . .

JACKIE. Oh, aye? Wantin' t' keep all the glory, are you?

ARCHIE. No . . . It's not that, man . . . It's the principle o' the matter . . .

JACKIE. Aye . . . all right, Archie . . . But you'll not be mindin' a bit o' competition, will you?

ARCHIE. Competition? How d' you mean?

JACKIE. Why . . . since the lads've come all this way . . . they might as well get a bit exercise . . .

ARCHIE. A see.

JACKIE. Then we can have a pair o' castles . . .

ARCHIE. Right then, Jackie . . . you're on . . .

Fade sound effects.

The sound of Big Ben striking. Crossfade to the interior of the House of Commons.

M.P. . . . And, Mr Speaker, I refer . . .

Cat-calls.

M.P. . . . Mr Speaker . . . I refer particularly to those men in the North East of this crippled country . . .

Jeers.

M.P. . . . Who are . . . Who are occupying themselves by constructing giant sandcastles . . .!

More jeers.

Perhaps . . . Perhaps the Prime Minister could . . . could reassure the House . . . that there're no plans in the pipe-line to make such an activity . . . official Government policy . . .

Laughter, jeers, footstamping.

Fade sound effects.

ARCHIE *and* BETTY's *sitting-room. There is 'romantic' music on the radio.* BETTY *stands by the window.*

BETTY (*slightly off*). My . . . it's a filthy night . . . (*Pause.*) Archie?

ARCHIE. Aye?

BETTY (*approaching*). What you thinkin' about?

ARCHIE. Oh . . . Just things . . .

BETTY. Like what?

ARCHIE. Like what the hell A'm goin' t' do with the rest of me life. That's all.

BETTY. Now, Archie . . . after all you've done these past few days . . .

ARCHIE. Aye, A know but . . .

BETTY. You're quite a celebrity now, you know.

ARCHIE. Aye.

Pause. BETTY *sighs.*

BETTY. A wish you weren't so bitter, Archie . . .

ARCHIE. . . . Bitter . . .? A've become so bloody bitter, A can almost taste it. (*Pause.*) All me life A've been in an' oot of work . . . scratchin' an' scrapin' . . . A would almost beg for work . . . buildin' sites . . . factories . . . warehooses . . . And then there was that time A went tank-cleanin' . . . D'you remember . . .? My God . . . What a job that was . . . Even Jimmy's never had t' do that . . .

BETTY. Things'll get better, Archie . . .

ARCHIE. Aye . . . mebbe . . . But will w' still be alive t' see it? A can remember what it was like for me father in the thirties . . . But it wasn't anythin' like this . . . This is much different . . . And it took a bloody world war t' get us out the mess that time . . . Still . . . It sounds crackers, A know . . . but in a way . . . buildin' that castle's helped get back me self-respect . . . And it's set me thinkin', an' all . . .

BETTY. Ee . . . well . . . A do know one thing, Archie . . .

ARCHIE. What's that?

BETTY. A'm really proud of you . . . A really am.

ARCHIE. Aw . . . Give over . . .

BETTY. Well I am. So there. (*Pause.*) A was thinkin' we might have an early night? There's nothin' on the telly and . . . and you must be tired after all that work . . .?

There is a radio announcement: 'And before our next programme we've just had a gale warning from the local weather centre who advised us that severe gales, force 9, veering north-west, increasing to force 10, are imminent. Owners of small boats are warned to take especial care and we advise that all moorings should be checked.'

BETTY. Archie . . . What you doin'?

ARCHIE. Goin' oot . . . that's what A'm doin' . . .

BETTY. But where?

ARCHIE. Now where d'you think?

Quick fade.

On the cliff tops later that night. ARCHIE, TOMMY *and* JIMMY *watch the sea destroy their sandcastle. The sound of waves in the distance.*

TOMMY. Well . . . We've certainly got a grandstand view from up here.

ARCHIE. Aye.

JIMMY. Dear, dear me . . . It's gettin' a right hammerin' . . .

TOMMY. Standin' up to it well, though . . . Considerin' . . .

ARCHIE. Oh, there goes another of your turrets, Jimmy.

JIMMY. Them battlements are still holdin' though.

TOMMY. Why, man, . . . that's British workmanship for you.

JIMMY (*chuckling*). . . . Aye . . . A'd like t' see the Japanese do better . . . (*Pause.*) Aye . . . it was a crackin' good castle that.

Pause.

TOMMY. Oh . . . there goes the last o' the turrets . . .

ARCHIE. . . . An' them battlements've started t' cave in . . .

TOMMY. . . . Looks like it's had it . . .

JIMMY. . . . All that work . . .

TOMMY. . . . Aye . . .

JIMMY. . . . Still . . . A've really enjoyed mesel these past few days. A really have. Haven't had so much fun since A was a bairn . . .

TOMMY. Aye. Me an' all . . . (*Pause.*) Have you not got any more ideas, Archie?

ARCHIE. A have actually . . .

JIMMY. What's that then?

ARCHIE. Well, Jimmy . . . You know how you spent half your life workin' in the ship yards?

JIMMY. How could A forget?

ARCHIE. Well, A've been thinkin' . . . Sandcastles seem a bit tame now . . . more for the bairns, really . . . Rather than a sandcastle . . . A was thinkin' more of a sand*ship* . . .

JIMMY. Now there's a thought . . . the biggest sandship in all the world . . .

ARCHIE. We might need a bit o' help mind . . .

TOMMY. Huh . . . that wouldn't be any problem . . .

ARCHIE. . . . We could dae it like a Second World War battleship . . .

TOMMY. Aye . . . Why not . . .? A'll get mesel doon t' the library first thing tomorra . . .

ARCHIE. A had another thought as well . . .

TOMMY. Oh, aye?

ARCHIE. A was thinkin' we might invite the Prime Minister t' come an' launch it . . .

The sounds of the storm grow louder. Fade.